STRADDLING WHITE AND BLACK WORLDS

Dr Paul Reck

STRADDLING WHITE AND BLACK WORLDS

How Interpersonal Interactions with Young Black People Forever Altered a White Man's Understanding of Race

The Black Studies Collection

Collection Editor
Dr Christopher A. McAuley

For Monique, Rennie, Coleman, and Evie, without whom this book would not be possible.

First published in 2023 by Lived Places Publishing

All rights reserved. No part of this publication may be reproduced, stored in a retrieval system, or transmitted in any form or by any means, electronic, mechanical, photocopying, recording or otherwise, without prior permission in writing from the publisher.

The authors and editors have made every effort to ensure the accuracy of information contained in this publication, but assume no responsibility for any errors, inaccuracies, inconsistencies and omissions. Likewise, every effort has been made to contact copyright holders. If any copyright material has been reproduced unwittingly and without permission the Publisher will gladly receive information enabling them to rectify any error or omission in subsequent editions.

Copyright © 2023 Lived Places Publishing

British Library Cataloguing in Publication Data
A CIP record for this book is available from the British Library

ISBN: 9781915734204 (pbk)
ISBN: 9781915734228 (ePDF)
ISBN: 9781915734211 (ePUB)

The right of Paul Reck to be identified as the Author of this work has been asserted by them in accordance with the Copyright, Design and Patents Act 1988.

Cover design by Fiachra McCarthy
Book design by Rachel Trolove of Twin Trail Design
Typeset by Newgen Publishing UK

Lived Places Publishing
Long Island
New York 11789

www.livedplacespublishing.com

Abstract

This autoethnography explores how young Black[1] persons shaped a White professor's racial consciousness and commitment to racial justice. Notwithstanding immersion in a "White" world and a whitewashed education, emotionally charged relationships with young Black persons spurred the author's vicarious understanding of Blackness. Foremost, the author's relationships with his Black godchildren and Black students provided access to a "Black" world and taught him important Blackness "lessons". Lessons addressing ability, threat, and guilt reveal Blackness associated with the worst, and discretion selectively exercised to Blacks' disadvantage. These lessons prompted the author to reflect on White privilege and the promotion of healthier interracial interactions.

Keywords

Blackness; vicarious experience; discrimination; expectations; discretion; threat; guilt; inequality; privilege; school

Content warning

This book contains explicit references to, and descriptions of, situations which may cause distress. This includes references to and descriptions of the following directed at members of some racial categories:

- Racial epithets, insults, and other verbal abuse (notably in Chapters 4–8).
- Physical abuse and threats of violence (notably in Chapters 5–7).
- Discriminatory and hateful nonverbal behavior (throughout the book).
- Substance use and abuse (notably in Chapters 3–4).
- Swear words or curse words (in Chapter 7).

Please be aware that references to potentially distressing topics occur frequently and throughout the book.

Note on racial terminology

This book employs a common Afro-American vernacular when referring to particular ethnic groups as "b/Blacks" and "w/Whites", as opposed to using one of the heavily debated descriptive terms for collectives in the social sciences such as "Black people"; "Black communities"; "White people"; and so on. Virtually every single person I identify in this book as "Black" uses the term "Black" to describe themselves racially and the term "White" to describe people of European ancestry.

Contents

Chapter 1	Seeds of my racial consciousness	1
Chapter 2	My miseducation regarding race and racism	9
Chapter 3	My re-education regarding race and racism	37
Learning objective Understanding how experiences shape racial consciousness		64
Chapter 4	Racially skewed expectations of intellectual ability	65
Chapter 5	Manufacturing Black threat	93
Learning objective Recognizing the variability of racial meanings		124
Chapter 6	Presuming Black guilt	127
Learning objective Recognizing expectations associated with Blackness and Whiteness		148
Chapter 7	Protecting White innocence	149
Chapter 8	Reflections on race privilege, power, and treatment	163
Learning objective Developing critical awareness of race privilege		189
Recommended projects and assignments		191
Notes		193
References		218

Recommended further reading 230
Index 231

1
Seeds of my racial consciousness

In the fall of 1971, I started kindergarten at age five at a predominantly Black elementary school in Longwood,[2] New Jersey, United States (US). I lived in a tiny, four-bedroom apartment in an all-White, working-class neighborhood that was on the periphery of Longwood's largest "Black" section in the northeastern part of town. This "Black" section contained a mix of working-class and poor families.[3] I was 1 of 3 White students in a class of 19; all of the other students were Black. Over the course of that first year of school, I became friendly with many of the Black students in the class as we worked together on various learning activities, played a variety of games, made art and crafts projects, went trick-or-treating together, and talked about the latest New York Knicks game or other programs we had watched on TV the night before. By the end of the school year, in June 1972, I had developed close bonds with my first group of friends, all of whom were Black.[4]

Although my family would move out of Longwood in August 1972, and I would attend virtually all-White schools in 3 different virtually all-White communities over the next 12 years, my first school experience in Longwood would play a profound role in shaping how I would come to think about race in later years.

At the time, I did not think of myself or my kindergarten friends in racial terms—my friends were just Tony, Wayne, Tamika, Ken, Elizabeth. Nevertheless, these friendships served as the basis for an early racial schema (cognitive map) I developed, in which connections to Black people not only were normal but also were fundamentally important. The primordial, visceral nature of these connections would give them a staying power in my mind even as I moved into virtually all-White social spaces in subsequent years. Limited, chance encounters with information relating to the Black experience and anti-Black racism in the US would powerfully resonate with me precisely because they were filtered through these early emotionally charged connections. Little did I realize at the time how these early childhood friendships would prime me to see the world in a more critical light. These early friendships laid the groundwork in later years for an emotionally rooted drive and openness to seek out Black friends, pursue an in-depth understanding of how race has comparatively shaped the lives of Black and White people, and ultimately to prioritize working to expose, combat, and dismantle systemic anti-Black racism.

My journey to developing a critical, self-reflective understanding of my own racial identity as a White person, and to continually seeking to understand racial meanings and challenge institutionalized racist policies and practices, has been, to a significant degree, inconsistent with my training as an educator. As educators, we are taught that in order to understand social phenomena, we must remain empirical, objective, neutral, and detached.[5] We are conditioned to not let emotions, connections, partiality, and subjectivity get in the way of what is largely an intellectual enterprise. However, while I certainly value developing an intellectual understanding of social reality, and engaging in empirical and analytic rigor, I see these pursuits as being inextricably connected to emotions, connections, partiality, and subjectivity. Indeed, my deeply personal, emotionally charged connections to young Black persons, beginning in Longwood, and for the past 39 years since I graduated from high school, have been the driving force behind my intellectual pursuits, not antithetical obstacles to them. Intense love, devotion, and a primordial sense of kinship that I feel for my four Black godchildren, Monique, Rennie, Coleman, and Evie,[6] as well as other young Black persons I have known, combined with limitless anger and outrage rooted in a fierce belief in fairness and justice, are the "oils" that power my intellectual engine. For instance, the cumulated rage that I have as a result of Rennie and Coleman's extensive history of harassment and mistreatment by police[7] has animated my teaching and research related to systemic racism in the criminal justice system. Once the intellectual engine has been activated, I then see empirical and analytical precision as potentially liberatory means of exposing and dismantling oppressive systemic practices.

On the surface, my journey to becoming a White person dedicated to understanding and upending anti-Black racism seems paradoxical and improbable based on the whitewashed miseducation about race and racism I received up through high school, and the virtually all-White spaces in which I was immersed from 1st through to 12th grade. The likelihood that I would embark on such a journey in this society also seems improbable in light of the ubiquity of racial misinformation, and the strong normative pressures to stay with your assigned racial "tribe". I, like my White peers, have been bombarded through the media and other sources with countless stereotypical messages suggesting that Black people are "violent", "criminal", "lazy", and want "handouts from the government".[8] We all cannot avoid internalizing and being subconsciously influenced by such stereotypical messages, and I have met many White people in my lifetime who have uncritically regurgitated this misinformation. When such stereotypical messages are coupled with racial segregation and a lack of vicarious experiences with Black people, these messages take on an even greater power and make White people even less inclined to try to establish connections with Black people.

There are also powerful normative expectations and pressures that discourage people from connecting with those outside of their socially assigned racial category. Contrary to fanciful notions that the US has become a "color-blind" society,[9] people are expected to stay within their socially designated racial category, and when they cross racial boundaries, they are invariably met with some type of negative sanction. I have experienced this on numerous occasions when I have been out in the world with both Black adults and Black children.[10] When I have been out at restaurants or other settings with Black adult females, I have received stares, looks of disapproval (e.g. eye-rolling), and sometimes disparaging comments,[11] mostly coming from White people. Likewise, when I have been out with Black children, I have sometimes encountered disapproval from some White people,[12] and, at times, from some Black people.[13] Moreover, it is not simply that we are expected to conform to norms regarding racial homogeneity, but that we must show allegiance to our assigned racial category. Those who stray outside of the category are viewed by others within the category as "traitors" who have abandoned the tribe. Interestingly, the high degree of racial segregation in this society renders these expectations and pressures to conform to racial homogeneity generally unnecessary. Most White people are presented with few opportunities to get to know Black people, and as a result it is easier to interact with other White people, and it feels more comfortable to interact with those who are familiar. In light of all of these factors, it is not surprising that we generally have not seen much cross-racial interaction between Whites and Blacks in the US.

In tracing the evolution of my racial consciousness in the face of all of these impediments to cross-racial interactions, this book emphasizes how opportunities to establish meaningful connections with young Black persons in various settings has been key to shaping this consciousness. In Chapter 2, I go through my extensive "miseducation" regarding race and racism up through high school to put into stark relief how significant these connections have been to the development of my critical consciousness about race and prioritization of race matters. Chapter 3 then addresses my "re-education" regarding race and racism, elaborating on the different experiences that I had after high school with young Black persons, and how my consciousness and commitment to understanding race and combating racism heightened as my bonds to young Black persons became more intense. I highlight in Chapter 3 how my connections to young Black persons opened a window into a parallel "Black" world to which I otherwise would not have been privy. Chapter 3 also elaborates on the process by which cross-racial mutual trust and respect was established, and how such trust and respect allowed for honest, unfiltered communication that was essential to my growth in terms of critical self-reflection.

Chapters 4 through 7 examine some of the crucial "race lessons" I have learned through my varied experiences with young Black persons as an adult. These "race lessons" address the substantive racial meanings associated with "Blackness" and "Whiteness", often in direct contrast to each other. Chapter 4 investigates expectations regarding ability,[14] and how educators typically equate "Blackness" with a low ability, and "Whiteness" with a high ability. This chapter highlights the role that educators' exercise of discretion plays in converting these assumptions into harmful outcomes for young Black persons, and serendipitous outcomes for young White persons. Chapter 5 explores the association of "Blackness" with threat, and, conversely, the association of "Whiteness" with the absence of threat. Chapter 6 delves into assumptions about Black guilt, whereas Chapter 7 probes assumptions of White innocence, and the elaborate, often hidden, efforts to preserve and protect such innocence.

Chapter 8 concludes with a self-assessment of how my experiences with young Black persons, and the various "race lessons" I have learned, have affected my own racial identity, how I see myself in relation to Black people, and how other people appear to view Black–White mixed-race groups. This chapter focuses in particular on examination of the privileges and power that I possess as a White person in this society, and the things that potentially qualify or neutralize such privileges and power.

This self-assessment concludes with some insights into the practices and skills that are necessary to develop and sustain healthy, meaningful cross-racial connections between Black and White people, even in a society scarred by over four centuries of systemic anti-Black racism.

2
My miseducation regarding race and racism

When I began attending public schools in New Jersey in the early 1970s, educators led me to believe that school was about learning the three "Rs" (reading, writing, and arithmetic). Unbeknownst to me, educators also were subtly imparting "lessons" about the fourth "R"—race. Throughout my 13 years of formal schooling between 1971 and 1984, I remained generally oblivious to the countless problematic tacit and subliminal messages about race that would shape my racial identity and racial consciousness as a "White" male, and contribute to an uncritical, convoluted understanding of Whiteness in contrast to Blackness. Overall, educators presented me with an antiseptic White world in which White superiority and dominance were natural and inevitable, and people of color were voiceless, extraneous, insignificant people sitting on the sidelines like Black lawn jockeys outside of a home in a White suburb. In order to put into perspective the significant influence that young Black persons have had on my racial consciousness throughout my adult life, it is important to first examine my formal and informal racial "miseducation" during my childhood and adolescence. In this chapter, I reflect back on the central features of this miseducation, focusing on the normative silence regarding race and racism, extensive omissions about the history, culture, experiences, and contributions of Black people and other people of color, gross lies and distortions when the topics of race and racism were addressed, and educators' discouragement of any meaningful study of race or racism. I also discuss how this miseducation was compounded by my immersion in almost exclusively White schools and White communities from 1st through to 12th grade.

Silencing and erasing race

Perhaps the most remarkable aspect of my miseducation about race was how little race and racism were mentioned during 13 years of schooling. Race was rarely discussed or even acknowledged, and generally was treated as something that did not exist. When topics relating to race or racism came up in some way, both teachers and students alike generally did not use race referents like "White" and "Black". For instance, lessons on slavery just referred to "slaves" and "slaveholders", downplaying the significance of race in structuring a system premised on race. Teachers and students, the majority of whom were White, were particularly likely to avoid using the term "White" to identify people. This failure to mark people as "White" reflected a consistent presentation of White people as the default whenever any topic was being discussed. In other words, we were taught to believe that any mention of "people" referred to **White** people. Paradoxically, the silence around race masked the many powerful subliminal messages that educators were imparting regarding race, often unknowingly.

Omissions and exclusions of Blacks' experiences in the United States

Along with the silence regarding anything dealing with race, there was scant mention of the history and culture of Blacks and other people of color[15] throughout my 13 years of schooling. Almost as if they had landed from another planet, Black people popped up in the curriculum on rare occasions. For instance, Black people briefly came into view when we addressed slavery and the Civil Rights Movement but then effectively disappeared into the hinterlands. It was as if Black people did not exist at other times in history. There was a dearth of information about Black history and culture even during Black History Month in the mid-1970s to early 1980s. Outside of superficial, tokenistic, fleeting mentions of Martin Luther King, Jr or Harriet Tubman during morning announcements in homeroom, when students generally were not paying attention, there was little said about Black people in the month of February.

While we learned little about Black people's culture and contributions, the most glaring omissions involved wide-ranging unconscionable policies and practices that White Americans have directed at Black people for four centuries. Consistent with the sanitized presentation of events involving Black Americans that I discuss below, there appeared to be an effort to hide the ugly truths of White brutality, savagery, and rapacity. For instance, we never discussed any of the massacres that Whites orchestrated and carried out against Black people in Cincinnati, Ohio, in 1829 and 1836, New York City in 1863,[16] Memphis, Tennessee, and New

Orleans, Louisiana, in 1866, Opelousas, Louisiana, in 1868, Colfax, Louisiana, in 1873, Wilmington, North Carolina, in 1898, Atlanta, Georgia, in 1906, Springfield, Illinois, in 1908, East St Louis, Illinois, in 1917, Chicago, Illinois and Elaine, Arkansas, in 1919, Ocoee, Florida, in 1920, Tulsa, Oklahoma, in 1921, and Rosewood, Florida, in 1923—among others (Anderson, 2021; Eldelstein, 2018; Francis, 2021; González-Tennant, 2023; Pitts, 2021; Schafer, 2022; Stephens, 2020; Tensley, 2021). Most notably, there was a virtually complete "whiteout" of Whites' ignominious behavior toward Blacks after slavery ended. There was no mention of the Black codes, convict leasing system, and sharecropping system, all of which effectively reinstituted slavery in the South in the post-emancipation era (Blackmon, 2008; Muhammad, 2010). We learned nothing about the wave of murder (e.g. lynchings), torture, and property destruction that Whites, including White local officials and police, unleashed on Black Americans after the Civil War under the auspices of White supremacist groups like the Ku Klux Klan (Januta et al., 2020; Mosvick, 2021). The racial caste system of Jim Crow segregation that was instituted primarily throughout Southern and border states in 1877 and remained in effect until the mid-1960s was mentioned only twice in 13 years—once in 8th grade and once in 11th grade—when the Civil Rights Movement was hastily brought up in social studies classes (Pilgrim, 2012). The vast array of voter suppression measures that Whites devised in the latter part of the nineteenth century to get around the Fifteenth Amendment to the US Constitution and to effectively deny Black people the right to vote were never discussed (Tensley, 2021). Through the omission of these post-emancipation practices, my classmates and I were led to believe that everything was fixed for Black people after the end of the

Civil War and the passage of the Thirteenth, Fourteenth, and Fifteenth Amendments.

Outside of brief coverage of the Civil Rights Movement, we learned nothing about Black people and the vast array of oppressive laws, policies, and practices that Whites established and carried out in the twentieth century to limit the life possibilities of Blacks and expand the life possibilities of Whites. In general, we learned about how the US emerged as a great nation with expanded opportunities for everyone and a burgeoning middle class by the mid-twentieth century. We were not taught that Black Americans were, for the most part, purposefully excluded from America's newfound prosperity and growth in the mid-twentieth century. We were taught that New Deal programs lifted Americans out of the Great Depression but did not learn that most Black Americans did not reap the benefits of New Deal legislation such as the Social Security Act and Wagner Act because the benefits of these Acts did not extend to agricultural and domestic workers—the two categories of work in which Black laborers were concentrated (Brodkin, 1998; Lipsitz, 1995). We also were led to believe that the GI Bill, through its educational- and employment-related benefits to veterans returning home after the Second World War, contributed to a vastly expanded and all-inclusive middle class. The systematic denial of such benefits to Black veterans was not mentioned, nor was the systemic exclusion of Blacks from labor unions and many professions (Katznelson, 2006; Sugrue, 2005). The omission of the assistance that the federal government disproportionately provided to those designated as "White", coupled with omission of the systemic discrimination Blacks faced in the private sector, left us with the impression that people of European descent earned their higher status in society on their own simply by working harder and showing more thrift than Blacks had done.

Perhaps most significantly, we learned nothing about the important role that the federal government played in creating a staggering racial wealth gap in the mid-twentieth century through its redlining policies and practices. I would only learn well after I finished high school about how the Federal Housing Administration (FHA), starting in 1937, and the Veteran's Administration (VA), beginning in 1944, engaged in blatant racial discrimination up through the mid-1960s by refusing to underwrite (insure) low-interest mortgage loans for prospective Black homebuyers (Brodkin, 1998; Katznelson, 2006, Lipsitz, 1995). Over 98 percent of those homebuyers whose mortgages were underwritten by the FHA or VA were designated as "White" (Race: The Power of an Illusion, 2003), yet this omission left students like me with the impression that those who had purchased homes had done so solely through their own hard work and thrift. We also learned nothing about how restrictive covenants and deeds, racial steering by realtors, and racial discrimination by White developers, White neighborhood associations, and individual White homeowners effectively prevented Blacks and other people of color from moving into suburbs created in the twentieth century (Massey and Denton, 1993). There was no mention of sundown towns—towns where Black people had to be out of town by dark in order to avoid threats of violence—which existed around the US and persisted up through the time I was in high school (Loewen, 2005). These latter omissions created a sense that virtually all-White suburbs, like the one in which we lived, had emerged naturally and meritocratically.

The omissions of history and culture relating to Black people were due in part to the textbooks we were assigned and in part to the decisions of administrators and teachers regarding what to teach and what to omit. All of the textbooks we were assigned had little information about events, experiences, and contributions relating to Black people, and virtually none of the textbooks included readings authored by Blacks. Most textbooks were filled almost exclusively with the exploits and contributions of prominent Whites such as presidents, generals, inventors, and authors. Even when textbooks included sections with writings by Black authors, my teachers skipped over them. For instance, the textbooks for both my ninth and tenth grade English literature textbooks had sections of writings by Black American authors, yet we were assigned none of these readings. In my tenth grade English class, a White classmate asked the teacher why we were bypassing the chapter on "Afro-American Writers", and the White female teacher casually replied, "We don't have time; they're not that important". Similarly, my teachers skipped covering Africa in my 9th grade World History class, and when I signed up for an elective on Africa in 12th grade, the class was canceled due to a lack of interest. Through these actions, teachers and administrators conveyed that perspectives, stories, and histories of people of African ancestry were irrelevant and not worth knowing, and, in doing so, they communicated that the White, European experiences and perspectives were superior and the center of the universe.

Misleading messages and lies about anti-Black racism and distorted portrayals of Whites and Blacks

While my peers and I developed an inaccurate and incomplete understanding of Whites, Blacks, and the operation of American institutions as a result of our educators' extensive omissions of this country's history of anti-Black racism, even greater harm was perpetrated on us by educators' misleading messages and lies about anti-Black racist practices, and distorted portrayals of Whites and Blacks in relation to each other, on those few occasions when race and racism was expressly addressed. Regardless of whether these lies and distortions, along with the omissions, were born out of ignorance, indifference, or conscious maliciousness, these inaccurate presentations of race and racism nevertheless reinforced and ingrained a message of White superiority and Black inferiority in unwitting students like me. I first examine the problematic ways in which educators presented anti-Black racism, and then turn to distorted and dishonest portrayals of Whites and Blacks.

Educators engaged in a variety of discursive strategies that all had the effect of downplaying the severity and significance of anti-Black racism in the United States. The sanitization of Whites' anti-Black racism was the most salient and most damaging of these discursive strategies.[17] Such sanitization was most evident when educators discussed the enslavement of Black people in the United States between the early seventeenth century and 1865. The message that teachers and textbooks conveyed was that slavery was not that bad—that White masters generally treated enslaved people of African descent "humanely" and living conditions were bearable. Educators and educational materials downplayed the unspeakable brutality of slavery through a variety of means. Educators used euphemisms to describe slave merchants' and slaveholders' practices. We learned that enslaved Africans were "brought" to the US, not "violently kidnapped", and that enslaved persons were "punished" by their masters for violating rules, not "whipped, beaten, and tortured" by sadistic, power-obsessed, egomaniacal captors (Walvin, 2018). Similarly, there were no graphic details or images presented of enslaved persons and the severe, dehumanizing conditions their captors forced them to endure, such as the backbreaking labor enslaved persons performed in fields all day in the hot sun and how such labor destroyed enslaved persons' bodies (Turner and Machado, 2019).

The horrors of slavery also were downplayed and obscured through significant omissions. We learned nothing about White male captors' systemic rape of enslaved Black women for over two centuries and the lasting emotional trauma of these rapes. There was no allusion to the constant state of fear of being violently assaulted by one's captors under which enslaved women, some enslaved men, and some enslaved children lived.[18] There was no mention of how enslaved persons were ripped apart from their families and had their own children forcibly taken from them, often to never be seen again (Brown, 2018). We also never discussed the overall psychic toll that slavery took on those enslaved. We were never asked to consider how having no control over one's life engenders anxiety, fear, and shame (Turner and Machado, 2019).

Educators also presented us with rationalizations that minimized the harrowing realities of slavery. For instance, teachers brought up how poor Whites in the South had tough lives and, in doing so, these teachers obscured the inhumane brutality that enslaved Black people endured. Educators also minimized slavery's harsh realities by saying virtually nothing about the numerous slave rebellions that took place and the wide-ranging acts of resistance by enslaved persons even in the face of significant, life-threatening obstacles to rebellion and escape (Blassingame, 1979; James, 1969; Turner and Machado, 2019).[19] By omitting any mention of this resistance and rebellion, educators led us to believe that enslaved persons must have been content with their lot, and that the conditions of slavery were not inhumane, violent, and traumatizing (Blassingame, 1979; Turner and Machado, 2019). We were left thinking that surely slavery could not have been that bad if enslaved persons did not resist in any way.

Besides sanitizing anti-Black racism, my educators downplayed such racism through the contorted ways that they framed events and the nature of such racism. In framing events inextricably tied to anti-Black racism, educators nevertheless found ways of presenting such events as being about something other than race. For instance, my teachers presented the Civil War as being primarily about a disagreement over "states' rights" as opposed to slavery (Flanagin, 2015). Similarly, a teacher's brief mention of the Draft Riots in 1863 framed such riots as opposition to the North's involvement in the Civil War, as opposed to White rioters' resentment of Blacks and opposition to fighting for Black freedom (Strausbaugh, 2016).

My teachers also soft-pedaled anti-Black racism by framing it as an individual problem rather than a systemic one. Teachers presented racism as largely based on individual prejudice and hate—that bigoted White people engaged in blatant acts of discrimination against Black people because they did not like them (Goldberg, 1997; Wellman, 1993).[20] For instance, when we briefly covered the Civil Rights Movement, my teachers made us believe that Black people's main obstacle to achieving equality was not White supremacist laws and institutional policies and practices that systemically perpetuated anti-Black violence and inequality but rather prejudiced individuals who were not nice to Black people. We were led to think that whatever discrimination Blacks faced in America was due to individual "bad apple" actors, such as Eugene "Bull" Connor, the Public Safety Director in Birmingham, Alabama, who facilitated, and in some cases ordered, violence against peaceful civil rights activists in the early 1960s. We were further convinced that once we got rid of these "bad apples", racism was over. My teachers steered clear of how systemic, structural racism—through laws and institutional policies and practices—severely limited Black people's opportunities, resources, and rewards. For instance, when we addressed discrimination against Blacks in education, we were presented with images of bigoted White individuals harassing Black children trying to integrate Little Rock High School in Arkansas, but we never addressed anti-literacy laws like Georgia's 1829 Anti-Literacy Act that made it a crime for Black people to learn how to read (Sherman, 2022) or segregation laws and policies that prevented Blacks from taking books out of libraries up through the 1950s (Sherman, 2022) and attending public universities until the 1960s (Clotfelter et al., 2015).

Another significant discursive strategy that minimized the significance of racism was situating any topics related to race within an overarching narrative of linear progress. Consistent with what Loewen (2005) describes, all of my teachers presented the United States as a great country that always was moving toward even higher levels of greatness in a steady upward trajectory of improvement and progress. We were taught that whatever problems existed in the US always were corrected, and once corrected, all was well for everyone in a society that was more advanced, noble, and progressive than before. We also learned that everyone in the US benefited equally from institutional improvements and advancements. This linear progress narrative was on full display when we finished discussing any topic related to racism. When we ended the material on slavery with a discussion of the Thirteenth Amendment, which abolished slavery,[21] the Fourteenth Amendment, which guaranteed due process and equal protection of the law, and the Fifteenth Amendment, which prohibited denial of the right to vote based on race, we were left with the impression that racism was completely over in the US and that Black people lived happily ever after. As alluded to earlier, this impression was exacerbated by the disappearance of Black people from the curriculum for almost a century's worth of time. Credulous students like me would have thought racism itself had disappeared because we only talked sparingly about Black people when there was some racist episode afoot. Similarly, when we finished material on the Civil Rights Movement with a short discussion of the Civil Rights Act of 1964, which prohibited discrimination based on race and color, and the Voting Rights Act of 1965, which outlawed discriminatory voting practices, we were effectively told once again that racism in America was over and done with, and that all was well for Black people and that we should move on to something else.

This narrative of linear progress conditioned students like me to believe in a story about America that simply was not true, and it upended our ability to think critically about social relations. Clearly, if racism was over after slavery and the US was continually getting better, then why were we revisiting it nearly a hundred years later? In presenting this narrative of racial progress, my teachers omitted three important sociohistorical realities. First, my teachers made no mention of the extreme backlash that has occurred in the wake of every effort to remedy racial inequality and injustice, however minor and incremental (Anderson, 2016). Any gains Blacks have made in attaining greater rights or opportunities have been met with virulent opposition from many Whites, who have intentionally and unrelentingly sought to roll back such gains (id.). For instance, as I noted above, there was a massive explosion of racist laws, policies, and violence in the post-emancipation period that continued well into the twentieth century in response to the end of slavery and the passage of the Thirteenth, Fourteenth, and Fifteenth Amendments (Anderson, 2016; Blackmon, 2008; Loewen, 2005). Likewise, the US Supreme Court's landmark 1954 *Brown v. Board of Education* decision was met with virulent opposition from powerful Whites in Southern states, who responded by shutting down public schools (Anderson, 2016), establishing private Whites-only "segregation academies" throughout the South (Carr, 2012), and passing new laws that kept in place racially segregated schools.[22] Similarly, in response to their efforts to end to the system of Jim Crow segregation, Black civil rights activists like Martin Luther

King, Jr were targeted by the Federal Bureau of Investigation's (FBI) clandestine Counter-Intelligence Program (Cole, 2003).[23] In addition, the passage of the Civil Rights Act of 1964 and the Voting Rights Act of 1965 triggered racially coded strategies to marginalize and disenfranchise Blacks (Anderson, 2016). Rather than ending racism, this 1960s civil rights legislation stimulated a whole host of cryptic and clandestine ways of perpetuating racial discrimination.[24]

Second, teachers failed to address how policies and practices can have long-term consequences that continue to wreak havoc on people's lives well after the policies and practices have ended (Turner and Machado, 2019). For instance, the FHA's and VA's redlining practices in the mid-twentieth century that effectively subsidized Whites' homeownership and denied such homeownership to Blacks, enabled White families to build up equity in their homes and pass on wealth to their descendants (Shapiro, 2003). This homeownership disparity is the principal source of the racial wealth gap in the US today, where the average White family has over ten times the wealth than the average Black family (Mineo, 2021). Likewise, centuries of racially-targeted violence, exploitative labor practices, crushed opportunities, and exposure to environmental hazards[25] have taken a psychic and physical toll on Black Americans long beyond the time of any corrective measures (DeGruy, 2017). To suggest, as my teachers did, that "all is well" and we should "forget about the past" after some blatantly racist policies and practices ceased,[26] or certain laws were passed, ignores the ongoing harmful effects of what has been done.

Third, teachers mistakenly led us to believe that everyone benefited equally from the expansion of the American Dream and institutional improvements and advancements. For example, we learned that the GI Bill's benefits helped to enlarge the middle class and enabled GIs and their families to live happily ever after in newly created suburbs. However, as noted earlier, systemic discrimination against Black GIs in the administration of benefits, coupled with discrimination by lenders, realtors, and developers, ensured that a middle-class life in the suburbs would be unattainable for Black GIs and their families (Brodkin, 1998; Katznelson, 2006; Lipsitz, 1995). Similarly, we learned that science, technology, and innovations were constantly improving the lives of everyone. For instance, advances in medicine, such as the polio and smallpox vaccines, had saved and improved everyone's lives. However, due the disproportionate percentage of Black people relegated to impoverished status in the twentieth century, as well as racial discrimination in the dispensation of care, Black people were not able to take advantage of improvements in health care to the same extent that White people were (Byrd and Clayton, 2001). Moreover, the sanguine image presented to us of a benevolent medical system that improved people's lives is belied by the numerous instances where the medical establishment used Black people as guinea pigs in life-threatening experiments like the Tuskegee Experiment (Washington, 2008).[27]

In addition to their inaccurate and misleading messages about anti-Black racism in the US, my teachers provided us with grossly distorted portrayals of White and Black people. My teachers presented White people foremost as benevolent, noble, and magnanimous. We learned about how the White male US presidents of the eighteenth and nineteenth centuries were great leaders and champions of freedom and democracy but nothing about how 12 of the first 18 presidents owned slaves (Andrews, 2019). We were taught about how Founding Father Thomas Jefferson was an architect of democracy and a drafter of the Declaration of Independence but nothing about Jefferson's view of Blacks as inferior, uncivilized "orangutans" who could never be assimilated (Jefferson, 1998).[28] We were told about how President Abraham Lincoln "freed the slaves"[29] and led the US through the Civil War but nothing about Lincoln's views that Whites were superior to Blacks and Blacks should be segregated from Whites.[30] There was a concerted effort to not only hide Whites' shameful views and actions, but also to play up "good" Whites like abolitionist William Lloyd Garrison as being representative of all Whites. This playing up of "good" Whites was tied to the narrative of linear progress. We were taught to see "good" White men beneficently granting rights to Black people throughout US history. In addition, we received a steady diet of inventions and other contributions of White men without any contextual information about how a minority of White men were afforded educational opportunities and had access to resources that were generally denied to everyone else up into the beginning of the twentieth century. The absence of this contextual information made it appear that these White men were simply more clever and industrious than everyone else.

My teachers also presented Whites as superior to Blacks and other people of color. This was most evident when the concept of Manifest Destiny was presented. Rather than critically interrogating this concept—which argued that White American settlers were authorized by God to expand across North America and seize land that belonged to indigenous peoples—teachers presented Manifest Destiny as having validity. We were taught that the White settlers believed that they were better at cultivating the lands belonging to indigenous peoples and therefore were justified in taking these lands. Consistent with the overarching narrative of linear progress, we came to believe that not only were these land seizures inevitable and natural, but that they benefited everyone in the long run by expanding the territory and infrastructure of a burgeoning mighty nation.

In contrast to their laudatory portrayals of Whites, my educators' portrayals of Blacks were highly denigrating. Many portrayals of Blacks characterized Blacks as infantile, dependent, docile, lacking agency, and largely irrelevant to the progress of the US. In part this was accomplished through significant omissions of Blacks' active struggle for freedom and social change. As noted above, we learned nothing about slave rebellions and Blacks' countless other acts of resistance during slavery and virtually nothing about Blacks' push for equal and fair treatment after slavery until the 1950s. Even when Black social change agents such as abolitionist Frederick Douglass and civil rights leader Martin Luther King, Jr were mentioned, they were presented as "exceptions". The failure to mention and emphasize the significant and courageous role that ordinary Black Americans played in the struggle for equality, often at great risk to their lives, left us with the impression that the majority of Black people lacked any agency, initiative, or fortitude.

In a similar vein, teachers' failure to discuss the significant contributions to the US that Blacks have made through their labor, ingenuity, and creativity fostered the belief that Blacks lacked agency and initiative. There was no acknowledgment of how, throughout US history, Blacks' labor in agriculture, industry, and service was central to the building of infrastructure and wealth in the US (Banerjee and Johnson, 2020). There also was no mention of Black people's numerous inventions and innovations, some of which have improved the quality of life and made life easier and others of which have been essential to Americans staying alive and healthy.[31] We were led to believe that every inventor looked like Thomas Edison and Henry Ford and were left with the impression that White men—and only White men—were responsible for innovations that enabled America to become a thriving and powerful nation. This presentation implicitly sent the message that Black Americans were free riders who benefited from the fruits of White men's creations. This was part of an overarching narrative that Black people were akin to "children" who depended on White "adults" to survive and function in American society.

When not presenting Blacks as infantilized dependents lacking agency, my teachers portrayed Blacks in a seemingly contradictory way as being wanton, reckless, out of control, and violent. While this latter portrayal contradicted the idea that Blacks were docile and lacked agency, it conveyed a problematic sense of "agency" that was aimless and destructive, much like that of unruly children having a temper tantrum. So while this portrayal of reckless, out of control Blacks challenged the idea of docility, it was nevertheless consistent with an infantilized portrayal of Blacks. This portrayal was evident when my teachers discussed the unrest in Black central cities in the mid to late

1960s. Teachers presented little to no context as to why these disturbances erupted around the country in the mid-1960s. Consistent with this context-free explanation, teachers described these disturbances as "riots" as opposed to "unrest" or "rebellions". This presentation conveyed the idea that these disturbances occurred in a vacuum and came out of nowhere rather than being the culmination of pent-up rage over Black people's abysmal living conditions, lack of opportunities, and poor life chances. By omitting any context or explanation for these civil disturbances, we were left with the impression that Blacks must have some inherent, natural propensity to engage in wanton, violent behavior like smashing storefront windows, setting fires, looting, and assaulting police officers.[32] Moreover, the coupling of this presentation with the extensive omissions of White mass violence and lynchings directed at Blacks in Tulsa and many other places caused us to cognitively equate Blackness with violence and Whiteness with order and tranquility.

In a similar manner, when teachers briefly addressed the Black Power Movement, it was not to show that Blacks had agency and fortitude to more forcefully demand changes to institutional structures that continued to trap many Black people in deplorable, impoverished conditions in the 1960s but rather to convey the notion that Blacks were gratuitously militant, violent, disrespectful of authority, and criminal. We were presented with the idea that "good" Blacks were those who, like Dr King, engaged in nonviolent, peaceful protest, and that the Blacks associated with the Black Power Movement were "bad" Blacks who unreasonably threatened violence to attain their objectives. Although Blacks were largely invisible in the curriculum throughout my schooling and presented as irrelevant and marginal to the progress of the US, when Blacks became visible, they were typically presented as pathological and ungrateful for whatever minimal opportunities they were afforded.

Compounding miseducation through immersion in predominantly White schools and communities

My miseducation was facilitated and compounded by my immersion in almost exclusively White schools and White communities from 1st through to 12th grade. I attended schools in three different, overwhelmingly White communities where Whites comprised 95 percent or more of the student population in the public schools. I had no Black students in any of my classes after kindergarten, and the high school, middle school, and last elementary school I attended did not have one Black student.[33] Outside of a few brief encounters, such as at basketball camps, I had almost no contact with Black people for the remainder of elementary school. These racially segregated, White insular community and school environments exacerbated the problematic lessons that educators were imparting by the effect they had on both teachers and students alike.

The absence of Black students in the schools I attended, and more generally the absence of students of color, made it more likely that teachers and administrators would present whitewashed content. The lack of any Black students in my classes made race less salient for educators, and so educators were less inclined to reflect on the racial dimensions of what they were presenting. Research shows that just having people of different races in the same room makes it more likely that people will think more broadly and consider more perspectives and vantage points (Vendantam, 2007). Without the presence of Black students, teachers and administrators also were less likely to receive any challenges, pushback, or demands for racially representative and accurate content from Black students or their parents or caretakers or to fear such challenges, pushback, or demands. In my 13 years of schooling, I observed only one White student—the student who questioned our tenth grade English teacher as to why we were skipping the chapter on "Afro-American Writers"—challenge a teacher on omissions or the factual accuracy of content relating to Black people. If there had been Black students present, it is more likely that teachers and administrators would have thought more about the race-related content that they were presenting and would have made more of an effort to devise a racially inclusive curriculum.

My teachers, almost all of whom were White, and my almost exclusively White student peers also would have developed a less whitewashed understanding of life in the US if there had been Black students from whom we could have developed some potential vicarious understanding of how Blackness shapes life experiences. As I note in Chapter 3, personal connections to Black people are fundamental to developing some type of vicarious understanding of Blackness. Without connections to Black peers, White students like me were more likely to develop a sense that our experiences were the same as everyone else's experiences, regardless of race. Moreover, the absence of Black students made

White students like me more inclined to believe that learning anything about Blacks or other people of color was not relevant to our lives in any way.

Cracks in the wall of miseducation and teachers' discouragement of studying race

Notwithstanding being fully immersed in schooling that comprehensively downplayed White racism and the experiences and contributions of Black people, there were some cracks in this seemingly seamless schooling experience that caused me to begin to think more critically about race and Blacks' experiences in the US. Toward the end of eighth grade, we were asked in my social studies class to write a term paper on a major topic in the US since the Second World War. Having just seen an article in a local newspaper about renewed efforts to create a national holiday recognizing Dr Martin Luther King, Jr, I chose to write about Dr King and the Civil Rights Movement of the 1950s and 1960s. Researching for this paper opened my eyes to the crushing inequities of Jim Crow segregation, but even more significantly, it revived the memories of all of my Black friends in kindergarten. As I became absorbed in the project, the injustices, indignities, and atrocities that Whites had perpetrated on Blacks through the elaborate Jim Crow system resonated with me so much because I personalized these injustices, indignities, and atrocities to my friends. I thought to myself, "How could such mean-spirited Whites do such horrible things to decent, innocent people?"[34] Following the completion of this paper, I became more sensitized to stories about racial discrimination directed at Black people.

For instance, after reading about a group of White people who harassed a Black family that had moved into a previously all-White neighborhood in a New Jersey suburb, I used this story as a basis for writing a fictional play called "Tones of Ignorance" for my ninth grade English class.

Near the end of high school, I had a number of seemingly minor chance experiences outside of my formal instruction in school that planted seeds for a further evolution in my thinking about race, particularly in terms of how Blacks and Whites were differentially treated in American society. In July 1983, after seeing an advertisement for a Monmouth County Social Services-sponsored program that took disadvantaged children out on recreational outings, I volunteered several times in that program. Most of the children in the program were Black, and I not only got to see the cramped apartment complexes where they lived but also learned a bit about some of the hardships their families were facing. Then on August 28, 1983, just days before the start of my senior year, I stumbled upon coverage of a gathering commemorating the twentieth anniversary of the March on Washington on the cable television channel *C-SPAN* and was moved by hours of speeches and commentary that highlighted how racial inequality was still deeply entrenched in American society. Around this time, I also began periodically watching the public affairs television program "Like It Is", hosted by Gil Noble, which delved into significant issues related to the Black experience.

While taking a sociology class in the fall of 1983 at my high school in which we barely scratched the surface of racial inequality, I approached the teacher after class and expressed my interest in learning more about racial inequality on my own. The teacher recommended that I read Jonathan Kozol's *Death at an Early Age: The Destruction of the Hearts and Minds of Negro Children in the Boston Public Schools*, which is an account of a fourth-grade teacher's experiences of teaching in a poor, overcrowded, nearly all-Black inner-city school in the 1960s. Reading *Death at an Early Age*, which vividly exposes how institutional racist practices systematically destroy the life possibilities of Black children, resonated with my own experience of attending a predominantly Black school in kindergarten. This book would serve as an inspiration for my numerous volunteer experiences working with Black children from low-income backgrounds after high school and prompted me to seek out other books addressing racial inequality. When my high school library was purging some of its collection, I grabbed a copy of *If They Come in the Morning: Voices of Resistance*, an anthology edited by Angela Davis that provides a scathing critique of how the criminal justice system repressively targets Black people. On a subconscious level, I think that my openness to learning about the experiences of Black people and racism in America, despite my immersion in a White world that largely ignored or downplayed these topics, was attributable in significant part to the emotional bonds I formed with my Black peers when I started school in Longwood.

As I moved into adolescence, the interest that I began to develop to better understand the significance of race and the experiences of Black people was largely discouraged by my all-White teachers, in both overt and subtle ways. After writing and doing a reading of my fictional play, *Tones of Ignorance*, which focused on the racial bullying a Black boy faced from his White peers after moving into a previously all-White neighborhood, my ninth grade English teacher's feedback to me and the class was that the story was "a bit contrived".[35] Afterward, I remember thinking to myself, "Contrived in what sense?" Was the topic of Whites harassing Blacks too fanciful for a fictional play assignment? Or was I being admonished in front of my peers for inappropriately suggesting that Whites are not necessarily "good" and "noble" people? Rather than using this as a teachable moment to talk about how the play's theme was situated in a much broader history of residential racial discrimination and exclusion, my teacher appeared to be dismissively telling me and my classmates that the topic of racism was not relevant and significant, and that we should focus on other, more important things. Moreover, this feedback appeared to be intended to sow doubt in my evolving understanding of Black people's experiences—that I must have been delusional to think that racism was still an important issue to discuss in 1981.

Similarly, when my tenth grade English teacher told the class that we were skipping the chapter on "Afro-American Writers" because "they're not that important", she was overtly stating that the perspectives and stories of Black people were not worth knowing.[36] By suggesting that Black authors could not teach White students any important insights about lived experience, this teacher was not only discouraging us from reading any Black authors, but was implicitly teaching us to devalue Black "messengers" as suspect. Moreover, by skipping the chapter on Black authors[37] and having us read only White authors the entire year, this teacher was instilling a sense of White superiority in us—that Black and other people of color had nothing to say that was worth White people's time.

Even the sociology teacher who recommended *Death at an Early Age* paradoxically appeared to discourage me from any further study of or involvement in addressing racial inequality through sarcastic references to me as a "bleeding heart liberal" and comments about the futility of changing anything in this society. Like my other teachers, this teacher was subtly conveying the message that as a White person, there were more fruitful and important things that I should be concerned about. Showing an interest in understanding race beyond the measly, superficial, token ways in which race was addressed in the curriculum was implicitly seen by these teachers as "getting out of my lane" and embarking on a trip to nowhere.

Most of ways in which teachers devalued the topics of race and racism and subtly discouraged study and discussion of those topics happened in very subtle ways that would elude an untrained observer. The most common tactic employed by teachers on those rare, unexpected occasions when race came up in some way was to quickly steer the discussion in another direction.[38] For instance, when the topic of South Africa came up in a current events discussion, a tenth grade social studies teacher quickly pivoted the discussion away from any critical analysis of South Africa's racial apartheid system and made the issue about how the United States and South Africa both shared an interest in stymieing the military involvement of communist countries like the Soviet Union and Cuba in Southern Africa. All of the ways—both subtle and overt—that my teachers discouraged any meaningful exploration of race had a cumulative effect of crushing whatever limited curiosity we White students may have had about race. More importantly, these subtle forms of discouraging any exploration of race and racism taught us to be passive citizens (Kamenetz, 2018). If racial inequality is not a problem—if everything keeps getting better and the house is not on fire—then there is nothing that we citizens need to do to address it. Ironically, at the same time that I and my White peers were being subtly taught to see Black people as lacking agency, our teachers were discouraging us, their White students, to develop any sense of agency with respect to racial matters. There was no need to write letters to our elective representatives or local newspapers, to protest, to volunteer, or do any of the things that good citizens are supposed to do in a healthy, functioning democracy (id.).

Key takeaways from my miseducation

My miseducation instilled many problematic ideas about race and racism. As a result of this miseducation, my peers and I internalized beliefs that racism was largely a nonissue in the 1970s and 1980s, that Black people were generally irrelevant and "Blackness" meant dependence or violence, and that Whiteness was the default standard of virtue, intelligence, productivity, and benevolence in a society always progressing to an even greater level of equality and fairness. The whitewashed education of distortions and lies my peers and I received while ensconced in a racially segregated, insular White world normalized Whiteness as being at the center of the universe in a taken-for-granted way and taught us to devalue and minimize the voices and experiences of anyone who was not White. Moreover, this miseducation predisposed us to view any efforts to correct the lies and distortions we were fed and seek the truth about race matters as suspect.[39] In addition, because we were conditioned to implicitly associate Whiteness with the US, we were more likely to see any criticisms about Whites as being "unpatriotic".

However, my ability to eventually break free from the lies and distortions of this miseducation and develop a more critically informed sense of racial consciousness and identity demonstrates that there are cracks in the foundations of any faulty presentation of reality and possibilities to see the world differently. My own experience is testament to the importance of having alternative spaces and opportunities that challenge the orthodoxy and uniformity found in some schools and communities. Television or radio programs, libraries, plays, and other venues can provide unexpected chance opportunities to see the world in an unfamiliar way and develop a more honest, accurate understanding of race and how it shapes the social world.[40] As I elaborate in Chapter 3, establishing close, emotionally intense bonds with people assigned to a different racial category also is key to developing a greater, more nuanced understanding of the ways in which people's ideas and assumptions about race can shape one's own life and other people's lives in variable ways. The close, emotional connections that I established with my Black peers in Longwood at the start of my educational journey helped to prevent me from fully buying into the whitewashed messages I received in the nearly all-White schools I attended afterward. As I discuss in Chapter 3, the many powerful emotional connections that I would form with young Black persons after high school would turn the cracks in the whitewashed understanding of the world I had been taught into wide chasms.

3
My re-education regarding race and racism

As I broke free from the intellectually stifling years of high school and moved on to college in the fall of 1984, my understanding about race and anti-Black racism was limited, naive, and filled with misconceptions stemming from an extensive miseducation that I could not grasp at the time. I remained a detached, distant observer of race and the Black experience as I started college. However, the chance opportunities and spaces in which I had begun to learn about the Black experience and history of anti-Black racism in the US and the reactivation of affinity I had had for my long lost Black classmates in Longwood made me open to and interested in connecting with Black people and learning more about Black history. Moreover, certain aspects of my upbringing and some key experiences early on in my college years contributed to a worldview that would be consonant or would heavily overlap with the worldview of many of my Black collegiate peers.

While the professors and the readings in some of my classes would no doubt help to alter the way I think about race and racism, the connections that I formed with Black college students at three different colleges and the young Black persons whom I got to know through two significant volunteer experiences played the most critical role in my "re-education" about race and racism. These experiences would reshape the lenses through which I see the world and would steer me toward seeking out and prioritizing connections with young Black persons for the rest of my life.

The influence of Black friends on my re-education

Of my network of just under 20 friends during my 4 years in college, only 2 of my friends were not Black. All of my closest friends and confidants were Black. At first glance, this seems remarkable in light of the "White" environment in which I had been educated and raised for the most part, as well as the fact that my college, Henderson, a small liberal arts college outside of Philadelphia, had a disproportionately White student body.[41] However, my nearly all-Black friendship network is not so counterintuitive when one considers the person I already had become by that first year and the opportunities that I had to connect with other college-going Black persons.[42]

During my first year in college a number of experiences buttressed my worldview in ways that would increase the likelihood that I would connect with some Black students. My nascent understanding of the Black experience prior to college advanced through my reading of Ralph Ellison's *Invisible Man* in an English class during my first semester, and through a volunteer experience in West Philadelphia that had a powerful effect on sensitizing me to the plight of the Black urban poor.[43] My inability to relate to the majority of people in my very ambitious, very privileged cohort of mostly White students at Henderson, many of whom had attended elite prep schools, made me feel like an outsider in ways that would resonate with some of my Black peers. The sense of entitlement that many of my White peers exuded further alienated me, as it ran counter to the fierce sense of fair play and rooting for the underdog and the most vulnerable that my parents had instilled in me. In addition, a nightmarish situation I had with the living conditions in my dorm,[44] and the College's unhelpful and insulting response to that situation, sharpened my critical skepticism of the fairness of institutions in a way that enabled me to better empathize and relate to some Black students' experiences with institutional unfairness. When all of these cognitive and emotional traits combined with the primordial sense of affinity, ease, and comfort in being with Black people that I had developed as child in Longwood,[45] it was likely that I would be amenable to taking advantage of opportunities to connect with Black students when such opportunities presented themselves.

Unlike high school, college presented me with numerous possible opportunities to form friendships with Black persons. Although Henderson was a predominantly White school, it had some type of joint enrollment with three other colleges and universities in the area—Bradford College, Stratford College, and Preston University—and there were many opportunities through off-campus activities and events. Some of the opportunities I encountered were by chance, whereas others flowed through established friendships and purposeful choices. Chance encounters led to meeting my best friend Calvin, who I met on a train out of Philadelphia when I was heading home for weekend in the fall of 1984, and my close friend Glenda, whom I struck up a conversation with on a walkway when we were both heading in the same direction after a class in the fall of 1986. Established friendships then set up possibilities for meeting and becoming friends with new people through a variety of means. Once I had established a friendship with a Black person, it became possible to meet and become friends with other Black people through that person's social network. This Black friend not only would be able to introduce me to other Black people whom they knew, but would implicitly vet me as an "okay" White person.[46] As I made Black friends, I also began to spend more time in "Black" spaces on different campuses, such as Black campus or cultural centers, which increased the likelihood that I would meet and get to know other Black students.

In addition, my network of Black friends increased the likelihood that I would meet new Black friends by shaping my thinking about race and racism in ways that would affect my social and academic choices. My friends provided access to an intellectual and cultural world I had previously known little to nothing about. Exposure to Black artists and musicians (e.g. Gil Scott-Heron) through my friends prompted me to attend Black cultural events on and off campus, and caused me to spend more time in Black social and cultural spaces off campus, such as a Caribbean club in Philadelphia. Most significantly, several of my friends introduced me to the writings of Black intellectuals, including Black radicals like W. E. B. DuBois and Walter Rodney, and Black feminists like Audre Lorde and bell hooks. We also would have long, late-night discussions about politics, racism, and other important social issues. Through these talks I learned about the Black Power Movement of the mid-1960s to the early 1970s and the FBI's violent, repressive efforts to destroy organizations like the Black Panther Party and assassinate or frame members of the movement for crimes. I also learned about how organizations and institutions at that time—including some of our own colleges— helped to prop up South Africa's apartheid regime. My friends made me think about racism in ways that were more vivid, complex, and unadulterated than anything I learned through more detached, distant, filtered presentations in classes.[47] My friends' real-life stories, unlike abstract, theoretical, or statistical information presented in formal lessons, could not be dismissed or rationalized out of hand.

As I increasingly came to look at the world through more critical racial "lenses" that my friends helped craft, I made academic choices that were consonant with further sharpening these lenses. In particular, I chose to minor in Afro-American studies as a complement to my sociology major, which made it more likely I would meet and befriend new Black students. For instance, I met and became friends with Thea and Celina after working together with them on a group project for an Afro-American literature class. Taking classes that focused on race and the Black experience also further developed my thinking through exposure to influential writings such as the *Autobiography of Malcolm X* and works by Toni Morrison.

My network of Black friends also, for the first time in my life, helped me to critically assess my own taken-for-granted privileges as a White person and to examine the lives of other White people through the prism of race. For instance, I began to think about how much easier it was for me as a White person to freely move about the world without being stopped and questioned by police.[48] I also started to scrutinize and think about how most White family members, friends, casual acquaintances, former classmates, and coworkers appeared to have no Black people in their immediate social networks and how they seemed perfectly comfortable with and oblivious to that social reality—it was not on their radar and they did not see anything wrong with living a racially segregated life. In addition, I began to notice and pay attention to the structure of social situations—who was and was not present, who occupied what positions, and what enabled some people to access and be successful in these situations and some people to be denied such access. For example, I became attuned to the extensive job connections that so many White people seemed to possess and the elite public and private school opportunities that White people were disproportionately able to secure for their children.[49] My critical reflection on Whiteness also was influenced by two significant volunteer experiences in college to which I now turn.

The influence of volunteer experiences in college on my re-education

The evolution of my racial consciousness in college also was profoundly shaped by two substantial off-campus volunteer experiences that brought me into contact with young Black persons. The first experience, which was sponsored through the "Kids Connection" program at Bradford, involved tutoring elementary school-aged children in the Germantown section of

West Philadelphia. I became involved with Kids Connection in October 1984 after hearing about it from a student who lived in my dorm, and I continued tutoring in the program through to the beginning of May 1986. Once a week a rickety van would pick up a group of mostly White Bradford and Henderson students and take us on a rather long (45 minute), bumpy ride into a mostly poor, all-Black part of Germantown, where we would meet elementary school-aged students who had signed up for tutoring at a run-down community center in the early evening. Each tutor was assigned a particular child with whom to work, although tutors would sometimes work with other children if their assigned child was not there, or if other children's tutors were not there. We mainly focused on helping the children with homework that had been assigned to them and practicing subjects in which they were struggling, but we also would do arts and crafts projects or play educational games with the children when we had finished going over their schoolwork. I was assigned a very shy, quiet seven-year-old named Erin, whom I would tutor for the next two years.

Tutoring Erin and some of the other children in their Germantown neighborhood opened up my eyes to a world that was so vastly different from the comfortable, safe, clean White suburban world to which I had become accustomed. Parts of the surrounding neighborhood were marked by boarded up, dilapidated buildings covered with graffiti, litter was strewn about in spaces, and there were some adult-age males hanging out on street corners who appeared to be unemployed. At some point in the fall of 1984, I remember walking past chalk marks on the sidewalk from a recent shooting (about a block from the community center) and being told by Bradford students in charge of the program not to "linger" in the neighborhood. Tutoring in this program vividly sensitized me to the plight of the segregated Black urban poor in the US and propelled me to understand the policies and processes that had contributed to this racial segregation and concentrated poverty.

Tutoring in the Kids Connection program also helped to challenge and dispel stereotypes about the Black urban poor that I had unwittingly internalized through my miseducation, through misinformation in the media, and from other White people I had known. It was customary for new tutors to meet the parents/caretakers of their assigned child at their home, so on my first day of tutoring I walked down to Erin's tiny row house, which was a couple of blocks from the community center, to pick up Erin and meet Erin's mother. Erin's mother and other extended family members who were living there[50] were pleasant and made me feel welcome. On this visit, as well as several subsequent visits to Erin's house, I was struck by the sense of family and connection throughout the neighborhood. People not only talked to each other, unlike in predominantly White suburbs, but actually looked out for and helped each other. On one occasion in April 1985, I came to tutor Erin but Erin did not show up at the center and was not at home. I asked a couple of neighbors if they had seen Erin, and they immediately organized an impromptu search party to locate Erin. I had been fed a steady diet of all of the pathologies that plagued poor Black urban neighborhoods, but the social bonds and concern for others that I saw far surpassed anything I had or have ever seen in any predominantly White middle- and upper-middle-class suburbs.

While I formed a bond with Erin over the course of two years of tutoring, I did not spend enough time with Erin to establish a relationship that was as substantial as the ones I would develop with young Black persons in subsequent experiences. The structured, mostly formal tutoring sessions at the center, coupled with transportation problems that caused us to miss some weeks' sessions, made it hard to build such a relationship. However, the regret I later felt in not returning to the program in the fall of 1986,[51] coupled with ideas this experience had generated as to how I could make future connections and experiences better for everyone involved, motivated me to seek out new opportunities working with young Black persons.

The second substantial off-campus volunteer experience I had interacting with young Black persons in college involved tutoring, mentoring, and engaging in recreational activities with high school students. After a number of my friends had graduated in spring of 1987, I was looking to get involved with young people in some way again. After speaking with someone at Henderson College's community service office, I started volunteering as a tutor and mentor at a branch house of the "A Better Chance" (ABC) program located in Avery, a town adjacent to Henderson, in September 1987. Eight of the nine high school student residents of ABC House in Avery were Black, and one was Latino. These students, who came from different cities all over the country, had been selected by the program to attend a highly ranked public high school in Avery.[52]

Over the course of the next year, I developed strong bonds with the ABC students, from whom I gained a richer understanding of race and how it structures opportunities and life chances. I initially started tutoring a couple of ninth grade ABC students once a week. Our sessions were largely limited to going over homework and discussing any issues they were having in school. However, as I began to spend more time at the house and had more space for informal interactions with the other students at the house, I was able to get to know and build up a rapport and a trust with all of the students at the house. Through a disarming combination of self-deprecating humor, empathetic listening, and validation of the students' thoughts and experiences, and a shared love of basketball, I was able to open up a channel of freewheeling, honest conversations with the students about a variety of topics, including race. My becoming an ally of the students—communicating that I was on "their side" and consistently following through in ways that backed up that talk—also was a significant factor in building that trust. The ABC students came to see me as a confidant and advocate,[53] especially as they griped about the three staff members at the house and some of the house rules, as well as incidents where they felt they were treated unfairly in school.

Perhaps the most critical factor though in establishing bonds of trust with the ABC students was getting involved in playing basketball with the students at various spots in the local area. I brought the students to play at the gym at Bradford College, played pickup games with them at courts at local parks, and eventually became a member of the ABC House's team that played teams from other chapters of the ABC program in the suburban Philadelphia area. In the course of playing ball together, we not only had a lot of fun and laughs, but we also had some of the most candid and profound discussions on race and other important topics. These deep, free-flowing discussions revealed to me the power of recreational spaces and activities. While some people had conveyed to me the idea that recreation and play were frivolous activities when I was growing up, I learned firsthand about how critical such recreation and play was to building trust and allowing nonthreatening space for open discussion.

I became particularly close to two 11th graders—Lamar from Chicago and Malik from New York—and they provided the most powerful insights about their lives back home and their experiences attending a predominantly White, middle- to upper-middle-class school in suburban Philadelphia. On one occasion when we were playing ball, a police cruiser rolled by, and Lamar commented about how he never felt free from threat. Lamar, who lived in the poorly constructed, crime-ridden Cabrini-Green public housing project in Chicago, discussed in detail an incident at Cabrini-Green in 1987 where he and his cousin were mistaken for members of the Bloods street gang because of their red Chicago Bulls jackets and were chased and shot at for six blocks by members of the Crips street gang. Lamar then stated that although he did not have to worry about gang members coming after him in the mostly "White" spaces of Avery, "I probably can't walk six blocks without cops rolling up on me and asking me where I'm going".

Malik, who was a member of the high school basketball team in Avery, also shared a number of compelling insights about race from his experiences on the team. While we were shooting baskets at a park down the street from the ABC House, Malik discussed how in the fall of 1987 his predominantly White high school had fielded its first ever all-Black starting five boys' basketball team. Malik noted that many White parents were in an uproar and were complaining to the coach behind the scenes and demanding that the coach start some White players. He then stated that a few weeks into the season, one of the starters, Dante, was suspended from the team for poor grades (even though that had not been an issue in the past), and another starter who was bumped for a less-skilled White player, quit the team. Malik used this example to make a broader point about how White people were okay with having some Black people around as long as things did not get "too Black", and as long as Black people were seen as not displacing White people from "their spots". In discussing Dante's suspension, Malik also noted that he noticed a pattern of Whites engaging in selective racial stigmatization. In general, Whites viewed Malik and other Black students at the ABC House as "good Blacks" based on the history and reputation of the program, whereas native Black residents of Avery like Dante were seen as "lazy" and less capable.

The discussions I had with Malik, Lamar, and the other ABC students gave me a more nuanced vicarious understanding of meanings associated with Blackness and made me reflect more on the intricacies of Whites' anti-Black racism. The richness of these discussions and strong emotional bonds that I formed over the course of nine months with the ABC students fueled a desire to actively seek out similar connections with young Black persons in my life after college. The modes of interaction, activities, and spaces that facilitated establishing a rapport and trust with the ABC students and that promoted open and honest discussions about race would serve as a useful template as I pursued interactions with young Black persons in the coming years.

Stepping into a Black world and becoming a godfather

In college, I went from a casual, distant observer of race to a guest or visitor in "Black" spaces on and off campus, and I received new, upgraded "lenses" through which to examine race and the experiences of Black people. Despite becoming more self-reflective of my White status, I continued taking my race for granted and at times lapsed back into the comfort of a White upper-middle-class world. I also was able to maintain somewhat of an emotional distance between myself and the young Black people I knew or had known. For instance, although I had established close bonds with the ABC students, I did not feel a sense of protective, parental-like responsibility for what happened to them. In 1993, five years removed from college, I would begin the process of a further upgrade of my racial "lenses", and a series of much more intimate, emotionally intense, and enduring experiences would take me from being a guest or visitor in Black spaces to becoming part of a Black family. I would no longer be a fleeting guest or visitor who could slip back into the comforts of a White world free from racial concerns.[54] In particular, the experiences I would have with four young Black persons who would become my "godchildren", as well as with their family members and friends, would forever alter how I understand Blackness, Whiteness, and my relationship to these two social constructs. The powerful emotional stake I would have in my relationship with these young Black persons would not only make race an even more powerful lens through which I would see and interpret the world but also would indelibly leave me with a fierce sense of responsibility rooted in kinship.

As I was switching career paths[55] to focus on becoming a teacher in the spring of 1993, I started tutoring a couple of women who were living at a transitional housing facility for recovering narcotics addicts along with their children in Ashford, New Jersey.[56] Feeling frustrated after one of the women I was tutoring was kicked out of the program after relapsing and another quit the program, I was preparing to leave the facility in July 1993 and try something else. Three new women, Deanna, Gladys, and Roberta, and their children moved into the facility in July 1993, and I started tutoring these women, all of whom were Black. I became friendly with the three women and built a trusting relationship with them in a short period of time. These women's children sometimes came by the room in which I was tutoring out of curiosity and began to engage me in conversations on the porch of the facility when I would arrive for a session. Seeing that the children seemed discontented with being confined to the house so much, I floated the idea of taking out six of the women's children to a local park. Deanna, Gladys, and Roberta liked the idea, and after obtaining approval from the facility's coordinators, I took the six children—Deanna's children Monique, age six; Rennie, age six; and Coleman, age nine; Glady's children Max, age nine; and Ian, age eight; and Roberta's child, Stan, age three—to a nearby park at the end of August 1993.

From our very first outing, there was a magical chemistry between the children, especially Deanna's children, and me. The children were full of seemingly endless energy and curiosity, effusively asking me every question under the sun as we ran around the park playing tag, throwing balls, frolicking on the jungle gym and swings, and laughing. There was an unexplainable joy about being together, and our instantaneous bonding made it feel as if we had known each other for years. In the months that followed, I regularly took the children out every week to parks, playgrounds, and beaches, and occasionally we went on seasonal- and holiday-related outings like pumpkin picking.

My involvement with the children increased by the early spring of 1994, after Deanna, Gladys, and Roberta all had graduated from the transitional recovery program and had secured subsidized housing in three different all-Black, lower-income neighborhoods in Ashford. That spring I continued to take the children to parks and other recreational spots in the area, but I also became immersed in the all-Black world of their neighborhoods, spending time at and in the vicinity of the children's homes. In particular, I spent even more time with Monique, Rennie, and Coleman, and the intensity of my emotional bonds with them strengthened. Unlike in my prior experiences with young Black persons, I felt a heightened sense of responsibility toward Monique, Rennie, and Coleman and began to take on the expanded role of a quasi-noncustodial parent, helping them with schoolwork, making sure they had sufficient food to eat and clothes to wear, and fixing problems that arose. When their mother Deanna relapsed by the end of the spring in 1994 and allowed a drug dealer to use her house for his distribution ring in exchange for her own supply of cocaine to consume, I was thrust into an even greater role of a protector of the children, like a mother lion defending her cubs. Moreover, as the children grew older and I became aware of racist obstacles that they were encountering in school and out in the world, my protective role became even more heightened. My college experiences had made me see personal choices as being political ones as well. In my own small way, I saw my protection and defense of my godchildren and other young Black persons whom I would get to know in the 1990s and 2000s as acts of resistance and ways of combating racist systems at the micro level.

In recognition of how I had taken on a more responsible, expanded role with Monique, Rennie, and Coleman, Deanna began telling family, friends, and strangers that I was the children's "godfather". Deanna's bestowing of this term was significant because it not only legitimized my relationship with the children and reduced any sense of confusion people might have about a White man being with three young Black children, but it conveyed that I had become a permanent part of the family, not just a visitor who would be here today and gone tomorrow. In becoming the children's "godfather", the trust-based, rock-solid ties that I had built with the children, their mother, other family members, and friends afforded me open, intimate, unfiltered access to a parallel "Black" world—like stepping through the looking glass—where I had a front row seat to observe how some Black people navigate the racial minefields of this society. Just as I often had opportunities to hear some White people's uncensored reflections and opinions, I now had a window into the unexpurgated thoughts, perceptions, and feelings of some Black people. As I became a member of the family and embraced my role, I now had countless opportunities to cultivate and fine-tune my vicarious understanding of Blackness in contrast to Whiteness through discussions, observations, and an inside view of subtle racist practices that often occur at a subterranean level beneath the radar. Moreover, becoming a fully engaged participant in cross-racial interactions with my godchildren enabled me to have a vantage point through which I could develop insights into the significance of race based on how other people reacted and responded to my being with the children.

My godchildren's willingness to candidly share with me insights about being Black and experiencing anti-Black racism in the decades after we first met in 1993 was made possible by the profound sense of mutual trust we had established. This trust was created through an array of interpersonal and social practices. My experiences with friends in college and with young Black persons in the Kids Connection and ABC programs had provided a foundation for some of these practices, but my intimate connections with my godchildren helped me to develop better cross-racial interpersonal and social skills. From the very beginning, being open and honest with my godchildren made it possible to freely talk about race. For instance, when Monique and Rennie asked me about slavery when they were six years old, I gave them a blunt, unadulterated account of Whites' sadistic greed and obsession with power and control. Rather than skirting or sugarcoating, I confronted these issues head-on, establishing a precedent for future discussions. My godchildren respected this honesty, which gave me credibility and authenticity in their eyes. As I had done with the ABC students, I also engaged in empathetic listening, which became increasingly important in facilitating brutally honest discussions about race and racism as my godchildren moved into adolescence. My validation of my godchildren's experiences when they felt that they had been slighted because of their race was critical in keeping an open channel of communication with my godchildren.[57]

Humor was another vehicle that assisted in having frank discussions about race. As it had with the ABC students, humor was a disarming way of putting my godchildren at ease. My self-deprecating humor communicated my own fallibility, and, in doing so, helped to break down status differences between us. Humor not only paved the way for talking about more serious things, but also humor became a direct way of addressing and mocking the absurdity of racism. For instance, when my godchildren were in high school in the early 2000s, we wrote and acted out a number of video skits, many of which poked fun at racist practices in the US.[58]

Being nonjudgmental also was an important interpersonal skill that allowed for open channels of communication. In the face of several years of highly tumultuous times involving my godchildren's mother Deanna's rock-bottom descent back into drug addiction in the 1990s, my godchildren's father's complete lack of involvement in their lives, and other family members' struggles with alcoholism, I consciously avoided any criticisms of my godchildren's family members so that my godchildren would not feel stigmatized for circumstances that were not of their making. I also was mindful of how any criticisms of family members coming from me, a White person, would tap into a variety of racial stereotypes about Black substance abuse and dysfunctional families dating back to the Moynihan Report in 1965,[59] which only would have amplified the race and class status differences that already existed between us and made frank discussions more difficult.

In addition to avoiding criticisms of family members, I engaged in several ways of reducing any potential stigma that my godchildren might feel due to the circumstances of their family members. I had discussions with my godchildren about the broader factors that contributed to addiction, and how addiction was fundamentally rooted in trauma.[60] We also had discussions of law enforcement's blatant race and class selectivity and hypocrisy in going after illegal drug activity in the so-called war on drugs. Moreover, I tried to minimize stigma by pointing out that problems like alcoholism were present in my extended family and common throughout our society. In doing so, however, I was careful to avoid statements that would convey that White people had exactly the same problems as Black people, or that I knew exactly what it was like to be Black and experience hardship and trauma in this society. As Oluo (2018) notes, comments by Whites who claim that they completely understand what Black people are experiencing or have had identical experiences can be very off-putting and alienating.

As I had learned in my experience with the ABC students, giving my time, actively participating in activities, and creating spaces for unfettered discussion were critical prerequisites to having candid discussions about race. Many of the things that I did with my godchildren over the years cost little to nothing (outside of the cost of gas to get to a particular destination). What mattered most was the time that I spent with them, and my active participation in whatever we did. Investing my time and being fully involved and present conveyed to my godchildren that they were important—that they were the priority. Creating comfortable spaces away from the struggles at home or at school—at the basketball courts, at the beach, or riding in the car on a trip—allowed for organic, often spontaneous, candid talks about race and other substantial topics.

Just as important as investing time and creating spaces in which to talk, consistency was invaluable in building the trust necessary for frank discussions about race. I not only made it a point to keep my word and follow through on visits with my godchildren, but I also circumnavigated many obstacles that made it logistically challenging in the mid-1990s to see my godchildren and stay actively involved in their lives. As a result of the volatility and tumult surrounding their mother's descent back into drug addiction, my godchildren's lives became highly unstable. My godchildren either were evicted or forced to move from homes as a result of fires and floods in several different towns in Monmouth and Ocean County between 1995 and 1998 and bounced around between family members in Landon, New Jersey and Washington, DC when Deanna was no longer able to care for my godchildren on her own. I had to persistently overcome Bible-thumping grandparents who viewed me with suspicion and rebuffed my initial efforts to continue seeing my godchildren in the fall of 1994, and I traveled down to Washington, DC to visit my godchildren when they spent parts of some summers staying with their older sister Teena.[61] My ability to have open, forthright discussions with my godchildren over the years has stemmed in part from their recognition of my unwavering devotion to them regardless of whatever challenges have arisen.

My displays of loyalty and unconditional love also factored into the trust that I built up with my godchildren. Even though I knew about Deanna's involvement with a drug dealer after Deanna relapsed in 1994, as well as the fact that my godchildren were missing school, I did not report Deanna to the Division of Youth and Family Services and did not cooperate with social workers who were snooping around in Ashford.[62] I also demonstrated to my godchildren that I was on their side and had their backs. My advocacy on behalf of my godchildren became more pronounced as they moved on to middle and high school, as I got involved in trying to fix problems or ensure better outcomes for them. During this period, I defended their interests through confrontations with teachers, guidance counselors, child study team members, principals, and other authority figures.

Efforts to make my godchildren comfortable also were crucial to facilitating open communication about race. I strove to meet my godchildren at least part way[63] by learning and taking an interest in Black culture, staying somewhat familiar with current pop culture, and by letting them have a say regarding which activities we did and what music would be played when we were in the car. I also sought ways to validate their Black racial identity by exposing them to Black-themed cultural events (e.g. festivals, plays, and poetry readings), "Black" spaces (e.g. Harlem), some of my Black friends, and Afrocentric books and other educational materials. While I also thought it was important to expose my godchildren to events and activities in predominantly "White" spaces in order to show that they had just as much a right to be in these spaces as anyone else, I often made sure that some of their Black friends or relatives also would join us so that my godchildren would feel less "out of place".

The extremely close bonds that I formed and strengthened with my godchildren over the 1990s and 2000s enabled me to get to know and establish close ties with several other young Black persons through them. I became involved with several of my godchildren's nieces and nephews, Rennie's friend Latanya's four younger siblings, and several of their friends. Between 2000 and 2001, I became particularly close to Monique's friend Chante, and her younger adopted sibling Tamika, who lived in Landon[64] and were being raised by Chante's mother's parents. When Monique, Rennie, and Coleman headed down to Washington, DC in June 2001 to spend the summer at their sister Teena's place, I spent a significant amount of time doing many of the things that I had done with my godchildren during the summer months—going swimming at a lake, playing outdoor games, going out for ice cream, seeing fireworks, going to fairs and festivals—with Chante, Tamika, their cousin Jamil, and their close family friend Cameron.[65] Analogous to my experience with my godchildren, the close trusting relationship I forged with Chante and Tamika led to candid talks about race and other issues of substance. Despite getting to know Chante and Tamika's grandparents, aunts and uncles, and other family members, and spending time at the grandparents' home, my ability to see Chante and Tamika was effectively cut off in September 2001 by their grandparents after their grandfather started having violent delusions connected to the onset of dementia.[66] This experience would be a very bitter lesson for me about how crossing racial barriers can sometimes run into intense resistance when such crossings upend people's deeply ingrained ideas of racial tribalism.

Still stinging from the loss of Chante and Tamika from my life, my sorrow and bitterness from that experience was somewhat neutralized by the introduction of Monique's best friend from high school, Evie, into my life in April 2002. In a short period of time, I became close to Evie, Evie's grandparents who were raising Evie,[67] Evie's other grandmother and great-aunts, and a variety of other extended family members. As with Monique, Rennie, and Coleman's family, I became an honorary member of Evie's family, and eventually became Evie's "godfather". Evie, who was 14 years old and living in Thornton in Ocean County when we first met, often went out with Monique, Rennie, and me, created and performed in video skits with us, and brought a sense of levity to any occasion through an incisive wit and sense of the absurd. I often sat and spoke to Evie's grandmother Estelle, sometimes for an hour or two, before heading out with Evie and my other godchildren. I also occasionally spoke with Evie's paternal grandmother Opal, and Evie's great-aunt Deirdre. Over the years they shared stories with me about experiences of racism that they had endured, which ranged from petty to life-threatening.[68] Unlike with Chante and Tamika's grandparents, Evie's grandparents and great-aunts, as well as other family members, came to see me as a fierce advocate for Black children and a protector of Evie.[69]

As Evie moved through high school, Evie became an integral part of my life, and my sense of responsibility toward Evie became the equivalent to that of my other godchildren. I took Evie to dance recitals, helped Evie with homework and to prepare for the Scholastic Aptitude Test, attended Evie's events at school, and had meetings with Evie's guidance counselor to complain about Evie's class placements and course schedules.[70] Starting in high school, but even more so in later years, Evie and I have had many deep discussions about the racism that Evie has encountered in different schools, the workplace, and public spaces. Evie, like my other godchildren, also has sensitized me more to the nuances of many Whites' often awkward interactions with Blacks, such as trying to connect with and relate to Black people through racial stereotypes. In addition, Evie, along with my other godchildren, has made me more attuned to the connections between race and class and to the subtle, hidden mechanisms that often contribute to racial inequality.[71]

Returning to the classroom and receiving new lessons about race and racism

In addition to my experiences with my godchildren, their relatives, and friends, my re-education regarding race and racism has been shaped by the many young Black persons I have met in a variety of different roles as an educator since 1993. Starting with my first full-fledged teaching experience at Royster High School (RHS) in Union County in 1994, the connections that I established with Black students, often outside of class, sharpened the critical lenses through which I perceive and make sense of the ways race shapes various phenomena and outcomes. Young Black persons at RHS and in other educational contexts sensitized me to a litany of educators' practices that conveyed racial meanings about Blackness and Whiteness. Black students brought racial dimensions of practices to my attention, made such dimensions more salient, and pointed out subtleties in differential treatment that often go unnoticed. More than any professors or professional mentors I had had, these students trained me to look beneath the surface of things and heightened my antennae to spot racial patterns and inconsistencies that others did not notice.

For instance, beginning at RHS, Black students apprised me of and made me highly attuned to practices that equated "Blackness" with "threat". As I discuss in detail in Chapter 5, these students' "lessons" about Black threat included the selective punishment Black students received for engaging in behaviors similar to that of White students, continual modifications to the school's dress and appearance code that appeared to target Black fashion styles, and the racial profiling of Black students by police and school officials after school. Black students at RHS also were the first of many Black students I would get to know over the years who pointed out ways in which educators went to great pains to preserve and protect White and American innocence. For example, I elaborate in Chapter 7 on how Black students at RHS brought to my attention how school officials tried to smooth over and cover up the apparently racist behavior of some teachers. Moreover, Black students at RHS and other educational contexts publicly raised contradictions and hypocrisies in curricula and presentations of history that sanitized or circumvented Whites' atrocities and shameful behavior, such as hiding the massive scope of the Native American genocide and obscuring that some immigrants (e.g. Africans) did not come to the US voluntarily. Black students at RHS also were the first of many Black students to alert me to some of the subtle mechanisms that contributed to an underrepresentation of Black students in higher-tracked classes.[72] It was through the Black students at RHS that I first became aware of some teachers' and guidance counselors' comments suggesting that Black students would not be able to handle the challenges of more rigorous classes. Black RHS students also made me acutely aware of the discomfort of being a Black student in majority-White classrooms.

As with the ABC students and my godchildren, I was rather quickly able to develop a rapport and build a sense of trust with Black students at RHS and in other educational contexts by making time for these students, empathetically listening to their concerns, and demonstrating that I was a sympathetic ally who was on their side. Many of these Black students were eager to share their race-related observations and concerns with me, and appeared to be starved of someone who would nonjudgmentally listen to them and validate their perceptions and feelings. These students appeared to be shocked to meet a White teacher who actually cared about Black students. Based on what these students shared with me, they were used to teachers—mostly White, but also some Black and other teachers of color—being hostile, dismissive, or indifferent to their concerns. Displaying my critically evolving knowledge about Black history and culture helped to bolster my credibility in the eyes of these Black students. My references to observations and experiences with Monique, Rennie, and Coleman also communicated that I was someone who could vicariously relate to and understand Black students' concerns.

In addition to having intimate access into Black students' insights and perceptions, taking on the role of an educator provided me a front row seat to peer "behind the curtain" and observe other educators' race-related assumptions and practices. Gaining the vantage point of an "insider" provided me with unfiltered access to subtle and covert mechanisms that systematically contribute to racially disparate outcomes, yet often go unacknowledged and undetected. In particular, as I note in Chapter 4, informal conversations with and observations of other educators provided countless opportunities to see how assessments and expectations of ability are tainted by race-related stereotypical assumptions. Beneath the veneer of seemingly colorblind practices, I came to see how deeply-embedded racial assumptions about students' ability often corrupt educators' decisions regarding class placement. I also was able to see how some educators—particularly White educators—had racially skewed assumptions about guilt and blame and came up with different attributions when explaining Black and White students' identical behaviors.[73]

Main lessons learned about Blackness and Whiteness

While there are many lessons that I learned about the racial meanings associated with Blackness and Whiteness throughout my "re-education" in the 1990s and 2000s, there are three main, overarching lessons. The first relates to default expectations people hold for young persons. In general, educators and non-educators alike generally "expect the worst" from young Black persons in terms of academic ability and a whole range of behaviors and "expect the best" from young White persons. The second lesson deals with discretion and how people exercise it in ways that disadvantage young Blacks and advantage young Whites. Young Black persons are heavily scrutinized, are expected to be perfect in the way they act, are pounced upon quickly for any perceived imperfections, are given no wiggle room to make mistakes or second chances to redeem themselves, and have to fight to be treated fairly even when they have met or exceeded standards of behavior or performance. In contrast, young White persons often are free from scrutiny, are permitted to be imperfect without any sanctions, typically receive second, third, and even fourth chances if they mess up, and are rewarded even when they have not met requisite performance standards. The third major lesson relates to the process by which meanings associated with Blackness and Whiteness are created. Such meanings are not inadvertent accidents or natural outcomes that effortlessly and mysteriously come into being. Rather, people spend staggering amounts of time and effort, often at a subterranean level, creating, maintaining, and reproducing racial meanings. I explore these lessons in greater depth in Chapters 4 through to 7, beginning with the racial meanings educators create and perpetuate regarding academic ability.

Learning objective
Understanding how experiences shape racial consciousness

The reader will understand and be able to articulate how personal and vicarious experiences shape a person's racial consciousness and racial identity.

- Identify examples of how personal experiences affected how the author thinks about race.
- Identify examples of how vicarious experiences affected how the author thinks about race.
- Identify how personal and vicarious experiences have shaped how you think about race.

4
Racially skewed expectations of intellectual ability

My relationships with many young Black people over the past four decades have provided me with many different "lessons" about race but specifically have taught me about the social meanings associated with "Black" and "White". One of the significant "lessons" I have learned about race relates to racialized expectations and assumptions about intellectual ability. The unmistakable crux of this lesson is that people, notably educators across a wide variety of schools and communities, associate "Black" with having lesser intellectual ability and potential, and "White" as having greater intellectual ability and potential. Through my involvement with and advocacy on behalf of my godchildren, my involvement with and advocacy on behalf of other Black children and their parents or caretakers, and my various roles within multiple educational contexts, I have had an inside look into how these racial meanings are created and shape students' schooling experiences, outcomes, and future trajectories. In the first part of this chapter, I examine in detail how educators construct and apply these racial meanings regarding ability in the context of class and curricular placement. Specifically, I address how educators' use of discretion works to the disadvantage of Black students and to the advantage of White students at both the low and high ends of the ability placement spectrum. I then analyze the ways in which educators convey lesser goals and aspirations for Black students.

Educators' discretionary class and curricular placement of Black and White students

Although educators claim that placement of children into classes and curricular programs is based on "objective" measures of ability such as standardized tests, the reality is that educators selectively apply their discretion in accordance with race-based assumptions at both ends of the ability spectrum. In general, I have observed or otherwise learned about numerous instances in which educators exercised discretion to the detriment of Black students and to the benefit of Whites. These discretionary placements have resulted in Black students being unjustifiably placed in "special education" and other low ability classes and kept out of higher ability classes such as honors and Advanced Placement (AP) classes, even when these students' grades and test scores warranted placement in such higher ability classes.

Educators' disproportionate placement of Black students in special education or other lower ability classes appears to have been guided by a default assumption that this is where Black students like my godchild Rennie, my friend Val's child Jared, Rennie's best friend Iggy, my friend Elvin's child Peter, my friend Mel's daughter Kira, and my friend Cate's son Mick belonged.[74]

While, as noted below, some of these placement decisions were based at least in part on some allegedly "objective" criteria such as test scores, other placement decisions occurred without any objective criteria or in the face of criteria that contradicted such low placement. For instance, Mick lacked any bad performances that would warrant placement in low-level classes, and Peter and Kira had high grades and test scores in their prior schools.[75]

A number of factors have bolstered these educators' default assumption that Black students possess lesser ability and have hastened these educators' decisions to assign Black students disproportionately to lower ability classes. Foremost, educators appear to have interpreted any indicator of poor performance, such as a low score on a standardized test, as incontrovertible evidence that Black students should be placed in low ability classes. Rennie, Jared, and Iggy all were hastily placed in special education after scoring low on one standardized test, even though their performance on other assessments was generally above satisfactory. In contrast, a poor performance on a standardized test or some other supposedly "objective" measure generally has not been a fatal blow for White students that results in placement in low ability classes. Rennie, Jared, and Iggy later learned that some of their White classmates had performed poorly on a standardized test, but these classmates' poor performances did not lead them to being recommended for or ushered into special education classes. For White students, educators have appeared to be willing to consider that environmental factors (e.g. distractions at home) may have contributed to these students "having a bad day", such that these poor performances should not be seen as the be-all and end-all assessment of their ability. Rather, educators have seen these White students, unlike their Black peers, as worthy of forgiveness and second and third chances, which in turn has enabled such White students to avoid special education and other low ability class placements.

Educators' view that one poor performance serves as a clear indicator of ability for Black students but not White students first became strikingly clear when a White male social studies teacher at Melton High School in Monmouth County went over the results of a pretest for two ninth grade world history classes while I was doing a practicum in the fall of 1993. In going over the results of the test, the teacher flagged several Black students who scored poorly on the test as being "at risk" and in need of "remedial work" but did not similarly flag several White and Asian students whose scores were comparable to those of the Black students. For this teacher, the Black students' poor performances on the test served as confirmation of these students' lesser capability. In contrast, when going through the White and Asian students' tests, the teacher casually said, "They'll be okay", suggesting that this pretest was an anomaly for the White and Asian students rather than irrefutable proof of their lesser ability.

While educators' considerations of how environmental factors might affect performance worked to the advantage of White students, educators appeared to weaponize environmental factors against Black students. Rather than being seen as circumstantial factors outside of school that could help put a Black student's poor performance into context, educators appeared to see Black students' family problems and other difficulties outside of school as signs that these students had lesser ability. If Black students exhibited any signs of poor performance, the stigma of family dysfunction provided extra confirmation that these students had limited ability and potential. For instance, when Rennie performed poorly on a standardized test,[76] educators at an elementary school in Seeburg saw Deanna's ongoing struggle with drug addiction not as something that was potentially compromising Rennie's ability to perform but rather as further "evidence" that Rennie did not have much raw intellectual ability. Similarly, Iggy's poor performance on a standardized test seemed to be conflated with Iggy's mother's struggles with drug addiction in Bedford in Ocean County, New Jersey. It appeared that any information about familial pathology activated broader racial stereotypes regarding Black people's ability and work ethic.

Educators' low assessments of Black students' ability were further bolstered by these students' parents' lack of involvement. Teachers and guidance counselors at both RHS, where I taught in the 1990s, and at Centennial High School (CHS) in Essex County, where I taught in the mid-1990s, selectively complained about how parents of struggling Black students were not involved in or supportive of their children's education. Educators specifically bemoaned how these parents did not come to Back to School Night, did not attend parent-teacher conferences, and did not otherwise do anything to facilitate their children's success in school. These educators seemed to assume that parents who did not help out their children with schoolwork or otherwise demonstrate concern about their children's schooling likely had limited ability themselves. In turn, these Black parents' children were assumed to have inherited this apathy and limited ability. Rather than seeing a lack of parental assistance as an environmental factor that adversely affected performance, educators perceived it as confirmation of students' lack of intellectual capacity.

Residential instability was yet another environmental factor that educators appeared to hold against struggling Black students. Educators appeared to view students as having lesser ability if their families moved a lot. For instance, between 1994 and 1998, my godchildren Monique, Rennie, and Coleman moved over a half dozen times, which disrupted their schooling and caused them to fall behind in school. Rennie and Coleman, in particular, struggled as a result of this transience and instability.[77] Rennie and Coleman failed to make up work related to absences, and performed poorly on assignments and standardized tests, which eventually led to both of them being held back in elementary school. Rather than viewing Rennie and Coleman's poor performance as being a straightforward result of the logistical difficulties they encountered in focusing on their schoolwork, teachers and guidance counselors with whom I spoke implicitly suggested that the boys' struggles were due to their stunted intellectual capability and their lack of interest in school. In making these assumptions about Black students, educators conflated specific performances with people's capacity to perform. Rather than seeing specific performances as being detrimentally affected by environmental conditions beyond the control of these Black students, such performances were seen as solidifying stereotypical assumptions about ability.

Holding residential transience against Black students appeared to be part of a broader tendency on the part of educators to presume that Black students possessed lesser ability if educators lacked familiarity with these students. Educators who were not familiar with Black students who had just moved to a district appeared to assume the worst about these students' ability and potential. As mentioned above, educators assumed that even new Black students, like Peter and Kira, who had demonstrated high records of achievement at their prior schools, had questionable ability. However, educators were even more likely to view Black students and their prior records of achievement with suspicion if those students moved from towns and cities that educators viewed as having low-quality schools and a variety of social problems. This was particularly evident at CHS, where teachers and guidance counselors were quick to distinguish "good" Black students who had come up through the two feeder towns' elementary and middle schools from "bad" Black students who had recently moved into these towns from nearby predominantly Black, disproportionately lower-income towns and cities. Black students who had come up through the towns' educational system were assumed to be capable, whereas Blacks students from these outside communities were seen as less capable, or at least as having suspect ability. For instance, Alexis, a Black ninth grader in one of my US history classes at CHS had been placed in a lower level track, even though Alexis clearly should have been placed in an honors-level class. It appeared that Alexis's guidance counselor and other CHS officials discounted Alexis's prior record of academic success because Alexis had newly moved from a predominantly Black city with a reputation for subpar schools. Even though CHS educators appeared to acknowledge the importance of environment in distinguishing Black students' educational experiences in CHS's feeder towns from those of outside of these towns, these educators nevertheless appeared to treat coming from a stigmatized community as a marker of having less intellectual ability and potential.

Once Black students were placed in special education or other low ability tracked classes, it was very difficult for them, their parents, and their advocates to convince school officials to move them out of these classes and into a higher ability class. After Black students were placed in these lower level classes, educators seemed to ignore or discount any subsequent improvements in these students' performances. For instance, despite general improvements in Rennie's and Jared's grades and test scores, it took Rennie over four years of wrangling, and Jared over five years of wrangling, to be moved out of special education classes. If Black students were pegged as having lower ability, then educators appeared to assess their performance through the prism of this low ability designation.

Black students' difficulty in moving out of special education and other lower track classes appeared to be due in part to educators' general tendency to view ability as being fixed for Black students. At every school where I worked or volunteered, I ran into educators who made statements implying that Black students' ability was effectively set and invariable. When I discussed the improvement of one of my students, Shaniya, a tenth-grade Black student in my US history I class at RHS in 1994, with Ms Beulah, my assigned student teaching mentor, Beulah scoffed at the idea that Shaniya could show such improvement. Beulah said, "[Shaniya] is a C, C+ student at best". Similarly, my social studies supervisor at CHS, Mr Mallett, rebuffed my praise for two Black students, Ervin and Mary, who had excelled in my American law and sociology classes during the 1995–1996 school year. After telling Mallett that Mary had written an outstanding essay and showed great analytical potential, Mallett sardonically dismissed my comments by saying, "[Mary] always has been a B- student, and she'll always be a B- student". Likewise, when I lauded Ervin's performance in the law class, and said how it was hard to believe that Ervin had performed so poorly during the first two years of high school, Mallett dismissively suggested that Ervin's performance in my class was anomalous. In contrast, educators never suggested that White students had fixed ability. Instead, educators praised White students who had shown improvement and growth. For instance, when I spoke with Beulah in 1997, Beulah spoke glowingly of Randy, a White student whom I had taught in 1994. Beulah stated that Randy had "come out of his shell" like David, another White student whom I had also taught back in 1994.

Besides their belief in Black students' fixed ability, educators' comments and advice to Black students appeared to play a significant role in keeping Black students mired in special education and other low ability classes. Special education teachers and other child study team (CST) members repeatedly told Rennie, Iggy, and Jared that regular classes would be "too challenging" for them. Likewise, these same educators told Deanna, Rennie's mom, Val, Jared's mom, Maya, Iggy's mom, and I that Rennie, Iggy, and Jared "were not ready" for regular classes and would "not be able to handle the work". In defending Rennie, Iggy, and Jared's continuing placement in special education classes, CST members typically adopted a tone that suggested they were being protective and compassionate. However, beneath the veneer of this ostensible concern for Rennie, Iggy, and Jared's welfare was a patronizing, belittling view of these students' capabilities. As Rennie noted years later, "[CST members] made me doubt myself; they destroyed my confidence in myself".

In addition to their discouraging rhetoric and advice, educators also helped to keep Black students locked into special education and other low ability classes through the pressured assessment environment that these educators created. CST members assessed Rennie, Iggy, and Jared's progress by collectively interrogating them in a room. Rennie described this environment as "intimidating" and indicated that it was hard to perform well because "I was on stage, and everybody was watching and waiting for me to slip up". Rather than objectively measuring these students' performances, CST members' assessment practices created a self-fulfilling prophecy in which Black students' performances were undermined in ways that were consistent with CST members' low expectations.

Educators' racially selectively discretion also worked against Black students and in favor of White students at the high-end of the ability spectrum. Notwithstanding Black students' high grades and test scores, teachers and guidance counselors routinely discouraged and fought against these high-achieving Black students from being placed in honors and AP classes or Gifted and Talented (G&T) programs. Both Monique's and Kira's grades and standardized test scores warranted being placed in honors classes, yet their teachers and guidance counselors told them and their parents that such classes would be "too challenging" and that they would have more success in regular classes. In contrast, Monique and Kira indicated that some of their White classmates, some of whom had lower grades and test scores, were encouraged to take honors classes.

Conversations with Black students in my classes at RHS, CHS, and Harper College in New Jersey revealed experiences of discouragement that mirrored those of Monique and Kira. Alexis, Anji, and Helen, ninth-grade Black students in my US history class at CHS, indicated that their guidance counselors advised them to take regular track classes despite their high grades and test scores. Alexis's guidance counselor told Alexis that the workload in honors classes would be too difficult to "handle". Ayana, Anita, Laquita, and Kenisha, the only Black students in one of my honors US History classes at RHS in 1994, bemoaned how much more difficult it was for them and other Black students to get into honors classes. Laquita and Kenisha talked about how their parents had to fight with school officials to be placed in honors classes, even though their grades and test scores were higher than those of most of their White peers. Ayana and Anita emphasized how Black students needed to "be twice as good as White students" to get into honors classes. Benita, a Black undergraduate student at Harper, discussed how Black students had to "be beyond excellent" or "exceptional" to get placed in honors classes at Benita's high school in the early 2000s. Benita noted that unlike the three Black students in Benita's honors classes, White students could be "nothing special, just good enough". Similarly, Bryan, a Black male undergraduate student at Harper, emphasized how the small percentage of Black students in honors classes at his high school, Baldwin High School (BHS) in Ocean County, had to be "superstars" in the 1990s. Bryan stated:

> You almost never saw any of us [Black students] in [honors classes]. They definitely weren't used to seeing the likes of me in honors [classes], but they really didn't

have any choice. I had such high scores; there was no way I couldn't be in honors.

Echoing Benita, Bryan insinuated that there was a racial double standard at BHS regarding who was and who was not encouraged to take honors classes. Bryan commented, "If you were White, you could get into [honors classes] by just being above average".

Bryan, Benita, Ayana, Anita, Laquita, and Kenisha's comments are backed up by what I observed in honors classes at RHS in the 1990s. There were between one and four Black students in the four honors US history classes that I taught at RHS, and all of them were A or A+ students. In contrast, there were a fair number of B and C students among the 20 or so White students in each of these classes. It appeared that White students who were "average" could be placed in honors classes, whereas Black students could only be placed in honors classes if they were exceptional. I observed a similar pattern at CHS in the mid-1990s and three other high schools where I taught as a substitute teacher in the late 1990s. I do not recall any "average" Black students being in any of the honors classes I taught or observed.

Educators not only appeared to discourage talented Black students from taking high-tracked classes but also seemed to bend over backward to find trivial justifications for keeping these students out of these high ability classes. For instance, Peter had grades and test scores that more than met the requirements for Marion's G&T program, yet he was told after applying that his score on the math section of a standardized test Peter had taken the year before was two points below what was necessary to be placed in the G&T program. In contrast, Peter's White male friend, Mike, who had lower test scores than Peter, easily got into the G&T program with no questions raised. Similarly, Laura, the oldest sister of Monique, Rennie, and Coleman, noted the battle she waged with Landon school officials to get her child Henry placed in honors classes. Laura indicated that school officials had shaved points off Henry's grade point average (GPA) to justify keeping Henry out of honors classes.[78]

Educators' rigid nitpicking in coming up with seemingly petty reasons for excluding Black students from higher tracked classes, and concomitant flexibility in placing White students in these higher tracked classes, appeared at times to be due in part to these educators' doubts that Black students could perform at a high level. This was most apparent when teachers questioned whether Black students had done their own work. For instance, Iggy's tenth-grade English teacher, who was White, returned a story Iggy had written with multiple words circled in red, and with a message at the top stating, "See me". Many of words that the teacher had circled were color-related, such as "shade" and "tint". When Iggy went to see the teacher, the teacher pointed at each circled word and asked Iggy what it meant. Iggy quickly defined each word and ultimately received an A grade for the story but was dumbfounded that the teacher doubted that Iggy knew the meaning of relatively simple words that Iggy had learned in middle school. Iggy also noted that none of Iggy's mostly White classmates at Baldwin Middle School (BMS) had had words circled in red on their assignments or had to prove to the teacher that they understood the words they used in their stories. While the teacher was dubious of the authenticity of Iggy's writing, the teacher apparently did not suspect that any of the White students' work was tainted by plagiarism or cheating.

In other cases, educators' reluctance to place Black students in higher tracked classes appeared to be rooted in their concern about appeasing White parents. Laura argued that two White teachers in Landon appeared to resent Laura's own success because "they didn't want [Black students] to excel over the White kids". Similarly, Laura alluded to Landon officials' concern about Black students displacing White students when Laura discussed the struggle to convince these officials to place Henry in honors classes. Laura contended that "[these officials] lessen the Black kids' chances to benefit the White kids and keep [White] parents happy". In the same vein, several veteran teachers at CHS told me that school officials in the district had struck an informal bargain with White parents to place their children in higher tracked classes to prevent these parents from pulling their children out of the schools. These teachers cited the trend of "White flight" in the district, where White parents were sending their children to private schools or moving to districts with fewer students of color, as the reason for this bargain. School officials were trying to stem this "White flight" by rewarding White parents who kept their children in the district's public schools.[79]

In addition to creating a high threshold for Black students to meet to gain entry into higher tracked classes, educators also appeared to exercise discretion to the disadvantage of Black students and to the advantage of White students in terms of whom they sought to remove from such higher ability classes. In general, educators appeared to scrutinize Black students in honors and AP classes more closely, watching for any signs of a drop in performance as a basis for recommending Black students switch into regular classes. Benita indicated that the handful of

Black students in honors classes at her high school in Illinois had to be "perfect", and that "teachers were looking to find some reason to kick [Black students] out [of honors classes]". Benita mentioned how a biology teacher suggested that Benita should consider taking the non-honors biology class after Benita missed an assignment. Benita also mentioned how a teacher pressured the only Black male student in Benita's honors geometry class to switch down to a non-honors class after this student failed a test. In describing this rigid standard that teachers appeared to selectively apply to Black students, Benita commented, "If we slipped up, they really weren't about any second chances for us". In contrast, Benita noted that "The White kids could flunk tests and nothing would happen to them". Furthermore, Benita pointed out that teachers were eager to help out White students who were struggling but saw Black students' struggles as a fatal flaw that warranted removal from class.

Amelia, a Black former undergraduate student at Harper College, echoed Benita's experience when Amelia recounted how Isaac, Amelia's child, faced pressure to drop out of honors English in eighth grade at a middle school in Middlesex County after receiving a C+ grade on an assignment. Amelia indicated that even though Isaac had a solid B average in the class and had had no other grades below a B, Isaac's White teacher swiftly and aggressively pressured Isaac to drop out of the class and requested a meeting with Amelia. At that meeting, Isaac's teacher suggested that Isaac would be more "comfortable" in a regular English class and argued that such a class would be a "better fit". Amelia also noted that Isaac was the only Black student in the class and that several of the mostly South Asian students in the class had grades similar to Isaac's, yet the teacher had not approached any of these students about dropping out of the class. Amelia suggested that Isaac's teacher appeared to be primed to "pounce" on Isaac for one subpar assessment. Moreover, Amelia described what appeared to be a racially selective pattern of teachers' and guidance counselors' provision of help to students at Isaac's middle school. Amelia stated:

> They expect the Indians to be in the top classes. My son's guidance counselor said, "Indians work so hard". They expect them to be successful. If [a South Asian student] messes up, they do whatever they need to get them up to expectations. When my son—the Black kid—messes up, they don't stay on [top of] him and try to help him.

As Amelia's comments imply, educators' racially selective expectations affect who these educators view as belonging in honors classes and being worthy of help. Moreover, Amelia's comments suggest that educators play an active role in creating self-fulfilling prophecies based on these expectations.

Consistent with Benita's and Amelia's experiences, Laura described that teachers in Landon expected Black students in advanced classes to be perfect and appeared to look for pretextual reasons to push Black students like Henry out of these classes. Even though Henry's standardized test scores placed Henry above virtually all of the honors class students, Henry's teachers viewed Henry as having suspect ability because Henry had an officially recognized disability that enabled Henry to receive accommodations. Laura indicated that Henry's teachers resented the fact that Henry received extra time on tests and needed to have an environment with reduced noise and distractions. Laura noted that the teachers would try to humiliate Henry in front of his classmates by publicly interrupting the class to send Henry to another room and implied to the rest of the students that Henry was getting some type of unfair advantage. Laura noted that this appeared to be part of a concerted strategy to drive Henry out of the class. Laura stated:

> [Teachers] don't want 504[80] students. They expect those students to be abnormal. They seemed to be looking for a way to get rid of him. It was like they thought, "Here is this [Black] kid who's getting some kind of favoritism, handout, who doesn't belong here".

For Black students like Henry, the stigma associated with having a learning disability appeared to tap into and activate teachers' stereotypical assumptions that Black students are less capable than White and Asian students.

Benita's, Amelia's, and Laura's accounts of the experiences of Black students in advanced classes suggest that educators had lingering doubts about Black students belonging in these classes and effectively viewed Black students' placement in these classes as being probationary and conditional. Any missteps by Black students or differentiation in any way appeared to make these doubts salient in educators' minds and confirm their low expectations of Black students' intellectual ability. Educators' selective scrutiny and nitpicking of Black students' performance in these advanced classes and unwillingness to work with and help these students appeared to be rooted in a belief that Black students had lesser intellectual capacity and did not deserve to be in these classes. These educators seemed to act as if it would be futile to try to promote the success of Black students in advanced classes because these students were not intellectually cut out for these classes.

Educators' expectations and goals for Black students: set your sights low

Educators' default assumption that Black students belonged in lower level classes, and educators' efforts to keep Black students out of higher level classes, were part of a broader set of practices revealing educators' low expectations of and goals for Black students. In contrast to educators' aspirations for White and Asian students, educators generally communicated that they did not expect Black students to achieve and do much in life. In particular, educators' words and actions conveyed that they did not expect Black students to go on to college. Educators communicated these low expectations and goals through their informal advice and comments to students and their formal curricular recommendations and programming decisions. When Black students demonstrated some record of achievement in high school and sought to go to college, educators encouraged Black students to set their sights low.

In general, educators did not encourage most of the Black high school students I have known to pursue a college education. In all of their years of schooling up through high school, Rennie, Iggy, Rennie's friend (and now spouse) Latanya, Coleman, Evie, Jared, and Isaac do not remember a teacher or guidance counselor ever encouraging them to apply to college. Any encouragement these students received to attend college came from me and other people **outside** of the formal schooling context.

Educators' failure to even mention college to these Black students was exacerbated by the minimalist goals that they articulated for these students. Teachers and other members of Rennie's and Jared's respective CSTs emphasized getting through the special education program and graduating from high school would be a major accomplishment. As Rennie has described, what mattered was just staying in school and getting a diploma. As discussed below, it did not matter to the CST members whether Rennie had the classes and skill set necessary to go on and be successful in college and meet other challenges later in life. Amelia described a similar minimalist insouciance when consulting with Isaac's high school guidance counselor to express concerns about how Isaac's grades and course selection might affect Isaac's chances of getting into college. When Amelia brought up these concerns, Isaac's guidance counselor matter-of-factly stated, "He's on target to graduate; there's nothing to worry about". The takeaway for Amelia was that school officials were content with the idea of Isaac having met the minimal standards necessary to graduate. These officials appeared to have no expectations for Isaac beyond that. In articulating these minimalist goals, educators appeared to sincerely believe that Black students and their parents or caretakers would be content with mediocre accomplishments.

Educators implicitly conveyed their expectations that Black students would not go to college through a variety of curricular and programming recommendations and decisions. For instance, guidance counselors at BHS routinely steered Black students, including my godchild Monique,[81] into its vocational program, where students would spend half of the day taking academic classes and then go to an off-site vocational school to focus on a particular trade. Although Black students accounted for less than three percent of BHS's student population, Black students constituted approximately a quarter of the students in BHS's vocational program. Guidance counselors played up how students would learn a trade and be able to start earning money right after high school but omitted how this program would sabotage students' ability to take classes that would enhance their chance of getting accepted into colleges.

Similarly, guidance counselors and other staff members appeared to disproportionately recommend the Junior Reserve Officers' Training Corps (JROTC) program to Black students at BHS in the 1990s. Although Black students constituted just under 40 percent of RHS's student population, they comprised over 70 percent of the students in the JROTC program in the mid-1990s. Students who participate in the JROTC program, which focuses on developing skills such as leadership, self-discipline, and responsiveness to authority, are substantially more likely to join the military than students who do not participate in the program (Baker et al., 2022). Although some high school students who go straight into the military eventually go on to college after they have completed their military service, educators' apparent steering of Black students into the JROTC program implicitly reveals that these educators see these students as better suited for the military than for college.

Besides disproportionately steering Black students into vocational and JROTC programs, educators also subtly conveyed their expectations that Black students would not be going to college by the courses they recommended Black students should and should not take. For example, even though Rennie and Evie had generally earned at least B grades in their science classes, their respective BHS guidance counselors advised them to not take chemistry because Rennie and Evie had both scored low on the science section of a statewide standardized test. Students who have not taken a chemistry class in high school cannot be admitted to the local community college, let alone regular four-year colleges. In cavalierly advising Rennie and Evie to not take chemistry, their guidance counselors indirectly expressed their belief that Rennie and Evie would not be going to college.

More broadly, as discussed in the first part of this chapter, educators' recommendations that Black students take less challenging classes insidiously revealed educators' low future expectations for these students. Rather than helping Black students to build an academic resume that would enhance these students' chances of getting into college, educators seemed more interested in moving these students through the system. Consistent with minimalist goals, educators adopted a "do what you need to get by" approach with Black students. Despite her high grades, Monique's guidance counselor initially discouraged Monique from taking honors classes at BHS. Likewise, Evie's guidance counselor advised Evie to take a basic English class instead of a college prep English class, notwithstanding Evie's A average in a prior language arts class.

Encouraging Black students to play sports was yet another subtle way in which educators expressed their expectation that such students would not be attending college. Although playing sports and involvement in other extracurricular activities in high school is commonly viewed as a way of enhancing a student's chances of getting accepted into colleges, the ways in which educators pushed sports on Black students, particularly Black male students, undermined these students' chances of going to college. For instance, although no teacher, guidance counselor, or other staff member **ever** mentioned college to Rennie and Coleman, staff members constantly tried to coax my godsons to play on BHS's football team. In trying to persuade Rennie and Coleman to play football, these staff members presented sports as something that they should put all of their energy into at the expense of concentrating on their academic schoolwork. Similarly, Bryan, who was a star basketball player for BHS, indicated that coaches and teachers talked about basketball not as a ticket to college, but as a potential ticket to playing professionally. Even though Bryan was also an accomplished student, Bryan felt that BHS staff members only encouraged focusing on playing ball.

Educators more directly conveyed their expectations that Black students would not be attending college through future- and career-oriented programming choices. For instance, Jared indicated how the coordinator for Marion High School's (MHS) special Eeducation program organized a trip to a car dealership to present the program's students with some possible "career options" once they graduated from high school. Jared noted that only the special education students at MHS, most of whom were Black and Native American, were taken to visit the car dealership. Jared further pointed out that none of the students in the special education program were taken on trips to visit any colleges, whereas the mostly White non-special education students at MHS were taken on several trips to visit colleges. MHS's officials' selection of students for these trips rather blatantly demonstrated a belief that Black and Native American students would be pursuing something other than college after graduating.

In a similar vein, coordinators of the afterschool program in Longwood for which I volunteered as a tutor between 2008 and 2010 displayed expectations that the program's mostly Black students would be pursuing something other than college in the future. When I proposed that Monique and another Black college student come in and do a presentation about college to the program's fourth and fifth graders, the program's coordinators balked at the idea, suggesting that the students would not derive much benefit from such a presentation. Yet the program's coordinators did not hesitate in organizing a presentation in which a local firefighter and police officer came in and talked to the students about their respective careers. The coordinators' amenability to this presentation, which involved two occupations that do not necessarily require a college degree,[82] and disinclination to my proposed college presentation, subtly conveyed that these coordinators did not envision these elementary school students attending college in the future.

Besides curricular, extracurricular, and career-oriented recommendations and programming, educators conveyed low expectations for Black students in more subtle ways. In all of the different schools I worked or visited in some capacity, I noticed a pattern of Black students, especially Black male students, sitting in the back of classrooms and seemingly disengaged. Teachers in these classrooms generally tolerated these students' disengagement as long as they were not disruptive. Sherry, the parent of a Black middle school student in Middlesex County, complained to a teacher after seeing almost all of the Black students sitting in the back of classroom. Sherry indicated that the teacher seemed to be indifferent to these Black students' disengagement. Effectively the teacher told Sherry that if the students did not want to pay attention "that was their problem". Rather than worrying about what Black students were getting **out** of these classes, educators seemed more concerned about just getting **through** the classes with as little disruption as possible.

Consistent with their general expectation that most Black students would not be attending college, educators typically discouraged Black students who were applying to college from aiming high. Even when Black students demonstrated a high level of achievement, guidance counselors and teachers often recommended that these students apply to a limited number of lower ranked state and private colleges. Despite a stellar record of achievement in high school, Monique's guidance counselor at BHS discouraged Monique from applying to highly ranked colleges. Similarly, although Bryan had a high GPA, and wanted to attend a major university, Bryan's guidance counselor at BHS heavily discouraged it, suggesting that Bryan should attend a lower-tier school to see if Bryan could "handle" college. Bryan's guidance counselor, like other educators, encouraged Black students who were applying to college to start at a community college. Bryan's guidance counselor suggested that Bryan attend a community college as a "stepping stone". Similarly, Amelia noted that Isaac's guidance counselor stated that "community college is a great place to start". Talking to other Black students and their parents/caretakers, I heard the same refrain. Guidance counselors and teachers urged Black students to exercise caution in applying to college, emphasizing that these students should make sure that they did not get in over the heads. Educators generally viewed the colleges that were "safety schools" for White students with similar records of achievement as being the "main choices" for Black students.

In addition to discouraging Black college-bound students from applying to higher-tier colleges, educators also encouraged these students to select less challenging majors. For instance, when Ayana met with a RHS guidance counselor in 1997 to discuss Ayana's desire to pursue a pre-medical program in college and eventually become a medical doctor, Ayana's guidance counselor recommended pursuing nursing instead. The guidance counselor suggested that pre-medical might be "too demanding", and that Ayana should first get accustomed to college before taking on more rigorous classes. Similarly, Amelia noted that after telling a high school mentor about wanting to major in mathematics in college, Amelia's mentor immediately shot down the idea as ridiculous. Amelia's mentor replied to Amelia, "Who majors in math?" Instead, Amelia's mentor suggested that Amelia major in communications. While educators ostensibly presented their downgraded curricular recommendations to Black college-bound students as protective measures to prevent these students from struggling in college, these recommendations were, in reality, paternalistic and condescending. Educators recommended less challenging majors because they appeared to believe that these Black students were not capable enough to handle more challenging majors. It is also possible that these educators, all of whom were White, had trouble envisioning

Black people working in academic and professional fields that historically had been overwhelmingly "White".

Problematic consequences of racially skewed expectations of ability

Educators' various practices based on low expectations of Black students' intellectual ability and high expectations of White and Asian students' intellectual ability have profound consequences on students' outcomes and trajectories and ultimately on the overall social order. These racially skewed practices often lead to educators providing Black students with less challenging work and cause Black students to develop less confidence in their intellectual ability. In turn, this makes it more likely that Black students will get turned off school and will be less prepared for college and the workforce. The often subtle, subterranean manner in which many of these practices occur results in such practices going unnoticed and makes it appear that the Black–White achievement[83] and wealth gaps happen seamlessly and naturally. As a result, Blacks' lower position in the US racial hierarchy is legitimized.

My observations and experiences suggest that the often vitriolic opposition to affirmative action in education is barking up the wrong tree. For the past half century, many Whites, some Asians, and most political conservatives have railed against affirmative action programs, arguing that such programs provide preferential treatment for less qualified Black, Brown, and Native people to the disadvantage of more qualified Whites and Asians (see, for example, Kroger, 2022). Yet I have observed or discovered a litany of practices in the K-12 educational system that amount to "affirmative action" for White and Asian students and significantly impair Black students' intellectual growth and academic success. Critics of affirmative action miss how educators' practices shape who is "qualified" in racially skewed ways between ages 5 and 18. K-12 educators' racially biased exercise of discretion in favor of White and Asian students not only hinders Black students' chances of becoming "qualified", but also undermines the success of Black students who, despite a minefield of obstacles, possess a greater intellectual ability and potential than their White and Asian peers.

Educators' general, watered-down expectations for Black students and lack of assistance to them in navigating the college application process and preparing them for other post-secondary pursuits is even more problematic due to racial disparities in family wealth and cultural capital. The average White family holds ten times more total wealth than the average Black family (Irving, 2023), which means that Black parents and caretakers generally have fewer resources and less time to assist their children with schooling and applying to colleges. Black families are also likely to possess a lesser amount of cultural capital—understanding of how institutions operate and how to navigate them—than White and Asian families due to the lesser likelihood that Black family members have attended college and are familiar with the process. This puts Black children at a disadvantage in navigating the college application process and other post-secondary undertakings. In light of these discrepancies, educators' lack of assistance means that Black children are more likely than White or Asian to confront a situation where they are receiving help from no one.

The low expectations that educators appear to hold for Black students dovetail with low expectations that authority figures appear to have regarding young Black persons' non-academic behaviors. Similar to how educators appeared to take any sign of Black students' poor performance as confirmation of educators' low expectations of these students, authority figures and civilians appeared to view any signs of young Black persons' misbehavior or any allegations of such misbehavior as confirmation of these authorities' or civilians' stereotypical view of Black people as being a "threat" or "guilty". I explore these latter racial meanings in depth in the next two chapters as I continue to elaborate on key "race lessons" that I have learned through my connections to young Black persons. The common threads of all of these "race lessons" are that people generally expected the worst from young Black persons, and then engaged in action that worked against the interests of these young persons.

5
Manufacturing Black threat

Of the many "race lessons" that I have learned through firsthand and vicarious experiences with my four godchildren, their friends and relatives, and other young Black people in a variety of contexts inside and outside of schools for the last three decades, those lessons relating to threat, safety, guilt, and innocence have brought racial meanings associated with "Black" and "White" into starkest relief. Unlike the clusters of race lessons relating to expectations of intellectual ability, lessons relating to threat, safety, guilt, and innocence often have been much more salient and indelible. By clearly demarcating differences between what it means to be "Black" and what it means to be "White", these latter lessons have played the most significant role in highlighting my own privileged social location as a White person. I explore how people have created associations of threat with Blackness in this chapter and then examine racial meanings associated with the related concepts of guilt and innocence in Chapters 6 and 7.

Since I began teaching criminology-related courses in 1998, I have emphasized the role that the media, politicians, and law enforcement have played in disproportionately focusing on and playing up Black criminality through demonization and dehumanization of Blacks charged with criminal offenses and ignoring and downplaying White criminality. Examining my godchildren's and other Black young persons' interactions with authority figures in schools and with police and White civilians in public spaces reveals that the process of constructing Black threat is much more complex and nuanced. Gender, age, spatial location, and the presence of White peers or allies all play a role in shaping perceptions of Black threat and affect people's treatment of young Black persons and young Black persons' perceptions of safety.

Gender and Black threat

While I have emphasized in my teaching that cultural meanings equating Blackness with criminality and deviance have disproportionately hinged upon Black **male** criminality and deviance, observations of and interactions with my godchildren and Black students in school suggest that the intersection of gender with race shape perceptions of threat in ways that are not as straightforward as they appear to be on the surface. Based on what I have observed and the numerous conversations I have had with my godsons Rennie and Coleman and other young Black males, it appears that authority figures, notably school officials and police, view Black males as being more threatening than Black females, particularly as Black males move into adolescence and young adulthood. As documented more fully below in my discussion of the intersection of age and race, I have observed these authority figures engaging in series of aggressive, proactive, formal social control measures that disproportionately target Black male individuals or groups. These measures, which include surveillance, containment of behavior and movement, excessive displays of force, and disproportionate punishment, suggest that authority figures view Black males as especially threatening.

My godsons and other young Black males have confirmed these observations by reporting a greater amount of scrutiny by and unsolicited encounters with police and other authority figures as well as more intense confrontations than those my goddaughters and other young Black females have documented. For instance, my godson Rennie, who is now 36 years old, has been stopped by the police over 60 times in his life, and my godson Coleman, who is now 39 years old, has been stopped by the police over 100 times. Both Rennie and Coleman have had police draw their weapons on them several times. In contrast, my goddaughters Monique and Evie have each been stopped by the police less than ten times in their lives, and have never had officers draw their weapons on them.

In explaining these gender discrepancies, Rennie, Coleman, and other young Black males have described how the intersection of Blackness with masculinity amplifies others' perceptions of them as being threatening. All of the young Black males I have known have emphasized that Whites in particular see them as hostile and threatening even when they remain calm. As a result of this default assumption of Black male hostility, any response by Black males to Whites in an encounter is interpreted by Whites as highly confrontational. For instance, my godson Rennie has noted:

> I'm already seen as hostile when I'm perfectly calm, neutral…. Me just responding, even if I'm calm and under control, to [a White person], that is seen as being aggressive, hostile.

Similarly, Omar, a former undergraduate student at Harper College, has observed:

> It doesn't matter how peaceful, respectful I am. Even if I am all polite, if I just pose a question to a cop, "Officer why am I being stopped?", or question my boss about something at work, they see me as angry, and things escalate real fast.

As a result of their concerns about how others, particularly White authority figures, might respond in an encounter, Black males have indicated that they are extremely cautious about speaking up. My godson Coleman has noted this point:

> If you try to speak up and defend yourself, the next thing you know is [Whites] are getting all bent out shape, and either ready to call the police or f*** you up somehow. It's not worth it.

Coleman, Rennie, and dozens of other Black males have indicated that this reticence to be assertive in an encounter is even more heightened when the other party is a police officer. As a result of others' perception of them as a threat, young Black males have uniformly conveyed that they do not feel completely safe and free in many spaces when they are out in the world.

Notwithstanding some of the practices that convey others' heightened association of threat with Black males, my goddaughters Monique and Evie as well as dozens of other young Black females whom I have known invariably have emphasized that others, especially Whites, see them as a threat. Young Black females consistently argue that they are gratuitously treated with hostility in a wide range of encounters on the roads and other public spaces, in stores, in school settings, and in the workplace. Monique and Evie have indicated that although they have had few encounters with law enforcement, they are typically treated as "criminals" and met with a high degree of hostility, particularly from White male officers. For instance, when Monique's car got buried in nearly three feet of snow when she was living in Middlesex County, New Jersey, a police officer berated her for not having moved her car yet, and threatened to fine and tow her if she did not move her car by later that morning.

Young Black females have noted that Whites in particular are likely to perceive them as "angry" or "having an attitude" regardless of how they actually act or what they say. For instance, my godson's spouse, Latanya, whom I have known since 2001, has remarked:

> [My coworkers] perceive me as being combative just by giving my feedback on a project.

Although Monique, Evie, Latanya, and other Black females have expressed less trepidation than Black males about speaking up in encounters with Whites, these Black females are more likely than Black males to describe feeling unsafe when they are out in public. Black females' heightened perception of being unsafe is rooted in a belief that society does not acknowledge and address the threats that Black females face. Monique has conveyed this point:

> [Black females] are in just as much danger as Black men, but we are not protected. Society doesn't acknowledge the violence and threat directed at us as Black females. Society perceives that Black males are in more danger,

and at least some people admit that. But the threats that Black females face are dismissed, ignored.

Monique's comments suggest that the greater visibility of the ways in which Black males are viewed and treated as threats helps to obscure both how Black females are viewed and treated as threats across a variety of settings, and in turn, this obfuscation makes Black females feel more vulnerable and in danger.

Age and Black threat

In addition to gender, age plays a significant role in shaping perceptions of Black threat. In general, I have observed that others' perceptions of Black young people as a threat dramatically increases as these young people move into adolescence and young adulthood. When I was with Black children between the ages of 4 and 13, there were some instances in which White individuals appeared to view Black children as being a threat to some degree but usually this sense of threat was muted. For instance, when I took my godchildren and/or their cousins, nieces, nephews, and friends to parks, beaches, museums, and other recreational spaces throughout their respective childhoods, some White parents or guardians communicated their discomfort with their White children playing with my godchildren or their Black relatives and friends. Typically, this involved these parents or guardians pulling their children away from these Black children when they were playing together. These avoidance efforts by some White parents or caretakers, which I observed on over a dozen occasions in Monmouth and Ocean counties in New Jersey in the 1990s and early 2000s, were often conducted as quickly, surreptitiously, and nonconfrontationally as possible.

I only remember a couple of occasions where a White parent removed a White child in a hostile, confrontational manner. One of these encounters took place at a beach in Monmouth County in August 1995, when Rennie and Monique, who were both eight years old at the time, were making a sandcastle with a White child who appeared to be the same age. The child's parent, who was visibly angry, stormed over to the child, yanked the child up off the sand by his upper arm, and publicly admonished the child, stating, "I don't want you playing with them". However, in most instances, White parents and caretakers removed their children with little fanfare, as if they were trying to avoid anyone accusing them of being racist.

Although, as discussed below, school personnel's formal social control practices conveyed a far greater concern about Black high school students' behavior, school personnel's social control efforts selectively and disproportionately targeting Black students in elementary schools suggest that these personnel view Black children as more threatening even at a younger age. This racially selective concern about Black elementary school-aged children was most evident when I observed two different afterschool programs in Longwood between 2008 and 2010 while working as a volunteer tutor. Both afterschool programs served students who were between third and fifth grade, but the racial makeup of the two programs was vastly different based on patterns of residential racial segregation. The afterschool program on the eastern part of town, which served approximately 90 students, was predominantly Black, whereas the afterschool program on the western part of town, which served approximately 80 students, was predominantly White.

The staff at the predominantly Black afterschool program exhibited a significantly greater concern with maintaining formal social control. Staff members instituted strict rules regarding talking and movement around the classrooms and continually berated and belittled children in the program often in very angry, animated, loud public ways. Staff repeatedly threatened the mostly Black children with punishment for talking and any other minor transgressions, often saying that they would inform the children's parents or that the children would be kicked out of the program.

In contrast to the austere, tense, highly punitive atmosphere at the predominantly Black afterschool program, the atmosphere at the predominantly White afterschool program was very laid-back. There were no strict rules regarding talking or moving about classrooms, and staff members were lenient even when students became somewhat rowdy. When staff members at the predominantly White program had a problem with a particular student, they privately talked to that student rather than trying to humiliate and make an example of that student in front of the other students. Unlike the staff members at the predominantly Black afterschool program, whose punitive surveillance and disciplining of students appeared to be driven by a fear that things would metastasize and spiral out of control, the staff members at the predominantly White program appeared to see children's talking and movement as normal and nonthreatening. The disparate treatment of Black and White children at these two respective afterschool programs suggests that even at an early age, school personnel view Black children as a threat and White children as harmless and innocent.

Authority figures' underlying perception of Black children as a threat became most pronounced in instances where the children were accused of violating some type of law. For example, in 1994, my friend Gladys's children, Max, age 10, and Ian, age 9, and Gladys's three nephews, Jamir, age 10, Nate, age 9, and Doug, age 8, were arrested for allegedly throwing rocks at cars and other minor acts of vandalism. All five children were Black, and Newbury, the town in which they were arrested, had a nearly all-White, middle-class population. When I went down to the police station with Gladys to secure the children's release, the two White Newbury police officers at the station described the children in highly threatening, menacing terms. The officers assumed that the children were part of a "gang" because they had "flashed gang signals" and "intentionally urinated" in the holding cell (as opposed to seeing it a fear-induced loss of control of one's bladder). The officers' attribution of malicious, adult-like intent to the children suggested that these officers did not see them as "children" who had engaged in some type of immature folly but rather viewed them as significant threats to the community.

Based on my observations of the childhood to adolescence transition of my godchildren and their Black cousins, nieces, nephews, and friends as well as the experiences of hundreds of Black adolescents at over a half dozen high schools, people's perceptions of young Black persons as a threat appeared to go up exponentially as Black children moved into adolescence. As Black students approached the end of middle school and the beginning of high school, I noticed that school administrators' and teachers' comments about Black students became laden with images of violence and criminality. For instance, when

I was a student teacher at RHS in 1994, I asked a White vice principal who was backstage at an event featuring an all-Black dance troupe from a high school in Passaic County, New Jersey about the whereabouts of my teaching mentor, and the vice principal sarcastically replied, "[The dance troupe members] have her tied up". The vice principal, along with another White staff member, laughed in a carefree way that conveyed their underlying stereotypical belief that Black adolescents were violent criminals. Other White staff members at RHS also made insouciant comments insinuating that they had expectations of criminality for young Black people, especially Black males. For instance, when I asked if anyone knew why Robert, a Black tenth grader in one of my classes at RHS, had been absent for the past week, a White teacher in the teachers' lounge half-jokingly remarked, "He's probably at the Union County Jail", and a White guidance counselor then chimed in, "That's where most of them end up" ("them" referring to Black males). Similarly, when I went to BMS in Ocean County to question the suspension of Coleman following a fight at school near the end of eighth grade in 1998, the school's White male vice principal stated, "If he keeps this up, he's going to end up in the Ocean County Jail".

In addition to comments conveying Black adolescent threat, such threat has been manifest by more aggressive, proactive, and punitive policies and practices targeting Black children once they reach high school age. School officials, law enforcement, and security personnel in particular have specifically targeted Black adolescents through heightened surveillance and proactive efforts to limit and contain these adolescents' behavior and movement. Two of the most notable examples of this magnified concern with Black adolescents were the "Watch List" compiled by school officials at CHS, where I taught in 1995 and 1996, and the "herding" practices of police officers outside of RHS in the mid-1990s and Longwood High School (LHS) in Union County in the mid-2000s.

The Watch List at CHS, which I became aware of while monitoring in-school suspension for the lunch period each school day, consisted of a list of 30 CHS students whom a CHS vice principal had deemed to be potential "discipline problems". School officials were alerting me and other CHS personnel to be extra vigilant of these particular students. After matching names to faces in CHS yearbooks and other sources, I discovered that all of the students on the Watch List were male and 28 of them were Black. Approximately one-third of the students at CHS were Black at the time, so the list clearly had an overrepresentation of Black students. During the course of the 1995–1996 school year, many of the Black male students on the list cycled in and out of in-school suspension. Regardless of these students' actual behavior, school personnel were likely primed to notice and react more harshly to any behavioral transgressions by these students.

Aside from the Watch List's glaring race/gender disparity of concern, CHS's school officials' elevated concern with Black male students' potential misconduct was all the more remarkable in light of a hazing incident involving four White male senior CHS students that took place in the fall of 1995 off school grounds. In this incident, these latter students, none of whom were on the Watch List, assaulted several ninth grade male CHS students with wooden paddles in a nearby park after school. The assaults came to light after several of the victims sought medical attention for their bruises. While CHS school officials did subject these four White male paddlers to several weeks of in-school suspension (during the lunch hour only), school officials made no effort to reassess and revise the Watch List. Although school officials had an egregious example of misconduct by four **White** male students that was substantially more egregious than any of the misconduct by Black male students, it had no effect on altering the assumptions of Black threat and White harmlessness undergirding the Watch List. Moreover, CHS officials' failure to reevaluate the appropriateness and utility of the Watch List was particularly striking in light of the sociopathic behavior that these four White males exhibited. In my own conversations with these students and assessments of essays they wrote (all four students were in at least one of my classes), none of the four displayed any sense of remorse, and all four took the position that their victims were responsible for bringing on their own victimization. These students' failure to appreciate the gravity of their actions appeared to be matched by school officials' and local authorities' nonchalance with respect to the assaults. Authorities declined to press criminal charges, suggesting that this episode was merely a prank, and all four students received recommendations and went on to college.

School officials also downplayed the four CHS White male students' paddling incident in another, more subtle way by treating the incident as an isolated, anomalous event. In contrast to incidents involving Black CHS students, which were treated as representative of **all** Black students' deviant propensities, this paddling incident was not seen as being representative of a generalized pathology among White students. For instance, in the aftermath of a major fistfight between two Black female CHS students that left both teens bloodied, administrators addressed a faculty meeting with innuendo that suggested there was a larger "Black" problem at the school. After the meeting, the principal, who was White, told me and a couple of other White CHS teachers that CHS had become an "urban" school as a result of an influx of Black students from nearby predominantly Black cities and towns in Essex County. Neither the principal nor any other CHS officials made any similar kinds of generalizations about White students following the paddling incident. Unlike CHS's Black students, who became more suspicious in school officials' eyes in the wake of the fistfight and other individual incidents involving Black students, CHS's White students did not face any heightened suspicion in the wake of the paddling incident.

Another notable, proactive effort to surveil and contain Black students was the practice of "herding" Black students that I observed outside of RHS in 1994–1995 and outside of LHS in 2005–2006. While teaching at RHS in the spring of 1994, several Black and Latinx students in one of my social studies classes complained about how they were monitored and harassed by police, particularly when they either walked home from school or ventured into the adjacent, nearly all-White town of Carson. These Black and Latinx students indicated that Royster police officers, both on foot and in patrol cars, "escorted" them down Oak Street and then Glen Avenue, as they walked home from school each day. Most of these students lived in the predominantly Black, lower-income Franklin Homes public housing project, which was located approximately one mile northeast of RHS. RHS had a student population that was roughly 40 percent Black, 55 percent White, and 5 percent Latinx and Asian in the mid-1990s, but approximately one-third of RHS's Black population lived in or near the Franklin Homes. While a disproportionate percentage of the mostly Black student residents of the Franklin Homes used Oak Street and Glen Avenue, some used an alternative route down Aspen Road and Edward Avenue to get home. Due to the limited provision of busing, most students walked to and from school.

On four occasions between spring of 1994 and spring of 1995, I observed a mostly Black crowd of students, usually in groups of four to six, walking down Oak Street, which is adorned with relatively large, single-family homes owned primarily by Whites. During each observation, there were at least two patrol cars and two police officers on foot from the Royster Police Department (RPD) that effectively followed the students down the street until they made it to Glen Avenue. Consistent with what my Black and Latinx students had described, officers admonished these student pedestrians for walking in the street and told them to keep moving when they lingered. A Black RHS student in my US history II class indicated that "[The RPD] treat us like we are cattle", and my own observations were consistent with this description. RPD officers appeared to be herding cattle down Oak Street as they closely patrolled the crowd of Black RHS students heading for home. I never observed any RPD officers following groups of White students heading in other directions away from RHS after school, but a gauntlet of officers routinely monitored Black students heading home on Oak Street.

In 2005–2006, I observed a similar phenomenon of police officers monitoring the movement of Black students walking home from LHS in Longwood when I was doing a research project on the police. The majority of Black LHS students lived in predominantly Black neighborhoods clustered in the northeastern part of Longwood, but LHS was located in the nearly all-White northwestern part of Longwood. Accordingly, a majority of LHS's Black students, who made up a little over a quarter of the LHS's student population, had to walk through "White" neighborhoods on their way home from school. On a half dozen occasions while doing ride-alongs with Longwood Police Department (LPD) officers, I observed a clear pattern of LPD following and occasionally interacting with groups of Black LHS students as they traversed all-White neighborhoods, especially down Sycamore Street. There were always two, and sometimes three, patrol cars monitoring the Black students' return home, whereas the one LPD patrol car positioned on the western part of LHS quickly dispersed after dismissal—the mostly White students heading home from the western part of LHS were not followed. Strikingly, six different LPD officers described their surveillance and unofficial escort of Black LHS students as "herding". As one LPD officer put it, "It's like herding cattle back into their pen".

Similar to what I observed after school outside of RHS, officers closely watched Black students and occasionally admonished them for walking in the street, walking on people's lawns, making excessive noise, and lingering too long. LPD officers shared with me that they felt compelled to engage in these racially selective practices in order to head off complaints from White residents along Sycamore Road and adjacent streets in the northwestern part of Longwood. The LPD's practice of "herding" Black students was consistent with the LPD's overarching pattern of policing of Blacks in Longwood, which featured LPD officers aggressively monitoring Blacks in any "White" spaces and efforts to contain Blacks to the northeastern "Black" part of Longwood.

Authority figures' enhanced, racially selective scrutiny of Black children as they moved into adolescence extended to other non-school-related spaces such as shopping areas. Up until they reached high school, my godchildren and their predominantly Black network of friends had never been approached by security personnel at a shopping mall in Ocean County. However, after they reached high school, security personnel began to home in on them, confront them, and question their presence and motives for being in the mall. On one occasion when Coleman was 18 and Rennie was 15, they went to an indoor shopping mall in Ocean County in 2002 and met, by chance, two other Black male friends and a Latinx male friend (all of whom were between 15 and 17 years old). After conversing with their friends for no more than two or three minutes, my godsons were approached by a White security guard who told them that they could not just "hang out", and that they had to disperse. A second security guard then showed up and told them they should leave the mall. Rennie presented the security guards with a shopping bag containing a newly purchased item to show them that he and Coleman had come to the mall to shop, and Coleman questioned why the officers were not stopping any of the larger, louder groups of White teenagers congregating inside of the mall. The security guards ignored Rennie and Coleman's mild protestations and continued to order my godsons and their friends to cease congregating. Reluctantly, my godsons and friends dispersed.

In addition to heightened surveillance, Black children faced unwarranted, excessive displays of force when confronted by authorities. For example, after a fight broke out between two White teenagers and someone called the police in Seeburg in Ocean County, Coleman and Rennie found themselves confronted by a situation in which half a dozen police officers drew their guns and began shouting orders at them. Even though Rennie and Coleman had nothing to do with this altercation, officers pointed guns at them as if **they** were the threat in this situation. Similarly, Keenan,[84] a 16-year-old Black student who attended a predominantly White high school in Bedford in Ocean County, indicated that he and another 15-year-old Black male companion were confronted by seven police cars when they were walking home a couple of minutes after an 8 p.m. curfew. Keenan, who was only a block from his home, was carrying a basketball and dressed in athletic clothes. Yet, as he noted, the police responded like he and his friend were "armed fugitives" who were on the "most wanted" list.

Besides authorities' disproportionate displays of force and more aggressive, proactive surveillance and containment efforts as Black children moved into adolescence, authorities' approach to young Black persons became increasingly punitive in racially selective ways. Some of these punitive practices were subtle, indirect, and symbolic, such as RHS's modifications of the school's dress and appearance code. Between the spring of 1994 and the spring of 1995, RHS officials continually revised the dress and appearance code, seemingly based on fashion styles disproportionately embraced by Black RHS students. RHS officials prohibited wearing large earrings like hoop earrings, chain necklaces wider than four millimeters visibly displayed over shirts and sweaters, work boots, and sagging pants displaying underwear. As Ayana, a ninth-grade Black RHS student in my US history I class in 1994 put it, "It's like [RHS officials] look to see what the Black kids are wearing, and then they ban it".

Other increasingly punitive practices targeted Black adolescents in a more direct and blatant way. As Black children reached the end of middle school and the beginning of high school, I observed school authorities subjecting them to harsher and more racially selective punishment. As discussed more fully in Chapter 6, Coleman was physically and verbally taunted by a group of White, mostly male, students at predominantly White schools throughout middle school and into high school and school officials began to frequently suspend him but not the White instigators in eighth grade when he fought back. Similarly, Sherman, a Black male who was the older brother of Rennie's friend Iggy, was subjected to racist taunts at a predominantly White middle school in Ocean County, and any time Sherman responded to such taunts, Sherman was suspended.

As Coleman and my other godchildren moved on to BHS, school officials' harsh, racially selective punishment practices came into stark relief through the staggering racial disparities in BHS's in-school suspensions. Notwithstanding that Black students accounted for less than three percent of BHS's student population, Black students routinely constituted over two-thirds of the students serving in-school suspension. My godchildren consistently described this racially skewed scene in BHS's in-school suspension room between 2001 and 2006. Evie recalled that 9 of the 12 students who were serving in-school suspension with Evie on a day in 2003 were Black. Evie added, "There were so few of us at [BHS], but you'd think we were the majority by looking at who was suspended". Coleman similarly indicated that the majority of students serving in-school suspension were Black. Coleman noted, "There was only one time when there were more White kids in the [in-school suspension] room". On one occasion in 2004 when I went to BHS to speak to Monique's guidance counselor, 10 of the 12 students sitting in the in-school suspension room were Black.

This overrepresentation of Black students serving in-school suspension at BHS appeared to be a result of BHS officials' racially selective exercise of discretion for minor transgressions. My godchildren indicated that BHS officials suspended Black students for minor things like shoving someone in the hall or cursing in class. Evie received an in-school suspension on one occasion for jumping up out of her seat on a school bus and chanting "woo hoo" when the bus went over a bump. In contrast, my godchildren bemoaned BHS officials' lenient treatment of White BHS students. Monique noted, "If you're a White kid at BHS, you won't get suspended unless you kill somebody". Keenan, the 16-year-old Black male from Bedford, noted a similar phenomenon at his high school. Keenan remarked that Bedford school officials routinely "cut [White students] slack", pointing out that White students regularly used profanity, vaped, and engaged in other violations of school rules without any consequences.

The increasing punitiveness as Black children moved into adolescence also was apparent at RHS. When I was at RHS during the 1993–1994 and 1994–1995 school years, I noticed a decline in the number of Black students in the ninth-grade classes as the year progressed. The major reason for this decline was the glaring racial disparity in referrals to the school district's alternative high school. As an RHS guidance counselor explained to me in 1995, Black RHS students were approximately three times more likely than White RHS to be referred to this alternative school. This "whitening" of RHS took place surreptitiously behind the scenes, as Black RHS students would vanish as if they had never attended RHS. However, unlike RHS's dress and appearance code modifications indirectly targeting Black students, these disciplinary referrals reflected RHS officials' direct targeting of Black students as threats.

Spatial variation of Black threat

While authority figures' view of Blackness as a threat increased as Black children aged, it also varied in complex ways by space. Looking across many contexts within and outside of schools, the degree to which mostly White authority figures and White civilians viewed Blackness as threatening foremost varied based on the racial composition of particular spaces and the meanings they attached to these spaces. In general, authority figures, the overwhelming majority of whom were White, routinely exhibited the greatest concern for the presence of young Black persons in spaces these figures appeared to demarcate as "White". In all the dozens of times that I played basketball with my godchildren and their friends and relatives after dark, the only occasion on which we were confronted by authorities to cease playing and disperse was on a late July night in the almost exclusively White shore town of Mansfield in Monmouth County in 2006.

That night, Coleman, Rennie, Monique, their friend Latanya, their niece Daisy, their nephew Roland, and I were playing basketball on an outdoor lit court adjacent to a Mansfield Fireman's Fair. As the fair was ending, we were approached by a Mansfield police officer and a couple of other officials at just before 10 p.m. and told that we needed to "pack it in" and disperse, even though it was routine for people to be out engaging in a variety of activities in this town on summer nights.

Keenan recounted a similar experience at this same basketball court in August 2022. Keenan and two slightly older Black male friends, all in their teens, were playing basketball on a lit public court when they were confronted by police at approximately 9 p.m. and told that they had to cease playing and go home. Keenan noted that the police followed Keenan's friend's car for almost a mile to make sure that they were leaving town. On their way out of town, Keenan saw several dozen White teenagers on bicycles or walking and noticed that the police drove right past these teens without a sideways glance.

Authorities' heightened concern about young Blacks' presence in "White" spaces was similarly evident in the aforementioned incident my godsons and their friends experienced at the shopping mall. The mall in Ocean County at which security personnel confronted my godsons and their friends was located in a predominantly White town, and most of its customers were White. Throughout their lives, my godsons have frequented shopping malls in more racially diverse areas with more racially diverse clientele without ever having their presence questioned in those spaces.

The most glaring example of authority figures' greater concern about young Black people in "White" spaces has involved police officers' motor vehicle and pedestrian stops. Almost all of the hundreds of Black adolescents and young adults whom I have known have complained about being unjustifiably stopped and harassed by police officers when walking or driving through "White" areas. Coleman, whom police officers have stopped over 100 times, and Rennie, whom police have stopped over 60 times, have been disproportionately stopped when driving or walking through towns with an overwhelmingly White population, especially in Ocean County. In the mid to late 1990s, Black RHS students indicated that they and other Black people were virtually guaranteed to be stopped by police if they walked or drove into Carson, the nearly all-White town that bordered Royster, whereas White, Asian, and Latinx RHS students made no such complaints about Carson police.

Similarly, in the 2010s, Black students at Odawa College repeatedly complained, both verbally and in writing assignments, that they, along with Black family members and friends, were stopped on the roads in the predominantly White town in which the college is located. These Odawa College Black students also bemoaned how they faced greater scrutiny from campus security officers when on campus. For instance, Curt, a Black Odawa College student, described several incidents in which a public security officer at the college's security booth selectively stopped and questioned vehicles with Black occupants. In one such incident in 2013, Curt and three other Black male students on the track and field team were stopped at the security booth and asked to show identification, while three cars with White male occupants were allowed to pass through the booth without providing any identification. Moreover, the public security officer then challenged the authenticity of the Black students' identification cards, further delaying their return to their rooms on campus. No White, Asian, or Latinx students lodged similar complaints when they discussed their experiences in dealing with campus security officers and police officers off campus.

Although Black students were subject to a more punitive approach (e.g. more likely to be punished for certain types of behavior, and to receive greater punishment than White, Asian, and Latinx students) in all of the schools where I have had some connection, the predominantly White high school BHS had the most punitive approach. As noted above, notwithstanding its minuscule Black population, Black BHS students constituted the majority of students receiving in-school suspension. As my godchildren and their Black friends noted, BHS also punished Black students selectively for minor things like talking or tardiness, suggesting that BHS officials viewed Black students' behavior as more of a threat.

Similar to authority figures, White civilians' apparent concerns about Black threat have been most pronounced in spaces that they have marked as "White". For instance, Rennie was confronted by an angry White resident shouting out of a window when playing ball with his two young sons in the grassy, inner, shared courtyard of a predominantly White apartment complex at which he was living in Eastmont in Mercer County in 2018. Rennie stated, "We were out there playing, and she was just upset, saying it was her grass and that we didn't belong there".

White civilians' concerns about Black threat have been particularly evident in public recreational spaces such as parks and beaches. For example, while riding a bicycle at a park in Hancock in Mercer County in 2021, Rennie, who was the only person of color in the park, was confronted by a White person who excoriated Rennie for riding too quickly and putting children in danger. Rennie contended that this person appeared to be emboldened to make these accusations by a group of White people who were nearby. Rennie indicated that at least a half dozen White people near him yelled "yeah" and started "ganging up" on Rennie as soon as this person confronted Rennie. After reviewing a video camera mounted on Rennie's bike, Rennie saw that this person's accusations all were baseless. Rennie was actually riding slowly past children and was alerting people either with the bike horn or by waving at them when he approached.[85]

Similarly, Rennie and my other godchildren have been confronted by hostile White civilians at or near beaches in Monmouth County on multiple occasions. For instance, in July 2022, Rennie was confronted by angry White middle-aged beachgoers in Oceanside in Monmouth County for playing paddle ball. Coleman had a similar experience in Oceanside in 2021 while playing Frisbee. In addition, on over half a dozen occasions, Whites yelled the epithet n***** from moving vehicles when I was with Coleman, Rennie, and Monique during the 1990s in three almost exclusively White shore towns in Monmouth County. We did not have such encounters in any other spaces.

White civilians' view of Black people as threats in "White" spaces appeared to be ratcheted up by anything that made Black people's "Blackness" more salient. For instance, Rennie argued that the White person who scolded him for riding his bike too fast in the park in Hancock was likely really upset about the rap music Rennie was playing out of the bike's speakers.[86] Playing this music made Rennie's "Blackness" more pronounced to this person and appeared to trigger whatever other stereotypical thoughts this person had about Black people. As Rennie pointed out, "Depending on the music I'm listening to, is how people respond".

It was clear in all of the aforementioned instances in "White" spaces that authorities and White civilians were not upset about behavior per se, but rather were upset about who was engaging in this behavior. On the night we were told to "pack it in" at the basketball court in Mansfield, I observed dozens of groups of young Whites riding bicycles, walking, and congregating outside. On other summer nights throughout the 2000s and 2010s I witnessed up to 200 rowdy, loud White youth congregating on the beach in Mansfield between 8:30 and 10:30 p.m. at night while a couple of police officers stood idly by on a street adjacent to the beach. At the same time my godsons were told to disperse at the mall in Ocean County, there were multiple groups of White teens loitering freely in the mall. Over the years I have observed White motorists speeding with impunity through the same spaces in which my godsons have been stopped by police, and White pedestrians have walked freely through these spaces without being confronted by police. The White person in Eastmont never took issue with the White children and adults playing in the courtyard, the White person in Hancock displayed no concern about White cyclists going fast or playing music, and the Whites on the beach in Oceanside had no problem with several groups of White teens and children playing Frisbee or tossing a ball nearby. All of these incidents show that what is really objectionable to authorities or White civilians is that Black people are doing things in these spaces.

Authority figures' and White civilians' racially selective targeting of Blacks in these spaces conveyed that these authorities and civilians saw Blacks as trespassing in spaces in which they did not belong. Authorities' and civilians' actions collectively sent the message that Blacks were not welcome in these spaces and should not use these spaces in the future. Authorities' and White civilians' objections to young Blacks' presence in "White" spaces invariably were tied to Whites' sense of entitlement to these spaces and the assumption that the presence of Blacks threatens Whites in some way. Authorities at the mall in Ocean County appeared to be worried that young Blacks at the mall might scare away White customers, whereas the presence of young Blacks at the beach was seen as threatening Whites' enjoyment of the space.

While authorities' perception of Blackness as a threat has been most unambiguous in spaces located in communities that are overwhelmingly White, the threat of Blackness in "White" spaces in racially mixed communities has been more complicated. Two critical factors that have affected the degree to which authorities treat Blackness as a threat have been the overall pattern of residential racial segregation in these communities and the extent to which cross-racial social ties have been normalized. As noted above, police officers in Longwood and Royster engaged in "herding" groups of Black students on their way home from high school in those two respective, racially mixed towns, but such "herding" did not occur in other racially mixed towns like Middleboro, where I also did ride-alongs with the police in 2005 and 2006, and Mayberry, where I taught at CHS in the mid-1990s. Unlike Longwood and Royster, Middleboro and Mayberry generally did not have highly racially segregated neighborhoods, and it was normal in Middleboro and Mayberry for young people to have cross-racial friendships. So authorities in Middleboro and Mayberry did not see Black young people as somehow being "out of place" and potentially "up to no good" if they were present or lingered in predominantly White neighborhoods in their respective communities. In contrast, authorities in Longwood and Royster assumed that Black young people generally had little to no connection to anyone in "White" neighborhoods because cross-racial social ties were not normative. This is why Royster police "herded" groups of Black students walking down the predominantly "White" Oak Street after school but generally ignored Black students walking down racially mixed Aspen Road.

Another factor affecting authorities' perceptions of Black threat has been authorities' concerns about pleasing Whites by catering to their interests in racially mixed spaces. This desire to appease Whites was most apparent at CHS and RHS. Although there was no "herding" of Black students in the neighborhoods outside of CHS, the existence of the Watch List demonstrated a greater focus on Blacks, especially Black males, as potential disciplinary problems within CHS. This greater formal social control of Black students through surveillance and punishment, appeared to be part of CHS officials' two-pronged strategy to prevent White parents from pulling their children out of the public schools. As I alluded to in Chapter 4, several CHS teachers indicated that school officials were concerned about stemming an increasing amount of "White flight", where White families were either sending their children to private schools or moving out of Mayberry and Sutherland, CHS's other feeder town, altogether as the schools became "Blacker". CHS officials' clamping down on Black students' alleged misconduct was one way of reassuring skittish White parents that any threat posed by an expanding Black student population was under control. As previously discussed in Chapter 4, Blackness also was seen as a threat to White interests in terms of class placements. To alleviate White parents' concerns about Black students somehow displacing their children, CHS officials disproportionately placed White students in higher track classes (e.g. honors classes).

Similar to CHS officials' apparent desire to placate White parents, RHS officials appeared to be driven by a desire to assuage White parents, and to convince these parents that their children would be "protected" at RHS. As noted above, RHS officials' ongoing war against any fashion/appearance styles disproportionately embraced by Black students seemed to be part of an agenda to assure White parents that RHS would not become "too Black". Moreover, just like at CHS, the majority of students who were placed in advanced ability classes were White, which, based on my own assessments of student work product at RHS, appeared to have little to do with actual ability. Like the officials at CHS, RHS officials seemed to be concerned with making sure that White parents would not pull their children out of a racially mixed high school and accelerate White flight.

In contrast to authorities' apparent perceptions of threat by young Blacks' presence in many "White" spaces and some racially mixed spaces, authorities generally engaged in an extremely laissez-faire approach toward young Blacks in predominantly or exclusively Black spaces. In the hundreds of times that I was with my godchildren in the predominantly Black sections of Ashford in Monmouth County and Landon in Ocean County, I never observed or heard about gratuitous confrontations with police or other authority figures. Likewise, in ride-alongs with the police in "Black" spaces in Longwood in 2005–2006, police kept their distance from groups of Black youths who were walking or congregating outside, in stark contrast to the aggressive "herding" of Black youths in the northwestern "White" section of town. In sum, authorities viewed young Blacks as "in place" in "Black" spaces and, as such, showed little concern for what these young people were doing.

The mitigation of Black threat through the presence of Whites

In addition to the racial meanings attached to spaces, authorities' and White civilians' perceptions of Black threat was affected by the presence of Whites accompanying young Blacks. In general, authorities' and White civilians' perceptions of Black threat were diminished or neutralized by the presence of either White peers or White authority figures. Authority figures were less likely to confront young Blacks when young White persons either walked or congregated with young Black persons. For instance, in both Longwood and Royster, police were most likely to "herd" all-Black peer groups.

The presence of White peers also helped to de-escalate volatile situations with authority figures. For example, in the incident in which police brandished guns on Coleman and Rennie when responding to a call about a fight between two White male teens in Seeburg, one of the two White combatants was able to effortlessly de-escalate and shut down the encounter. As the situation quickly spiraled out of control, this White combatant was able to abruptly defuse the situation by dropping a pipe and telling the officers that they were just roughhousing. The officers backed off as soon as this White teen told the officers that there was nothing about which they should be concerned.

The presence of at least one White authority figure also has appeared to temper authority figures' and White civilians' perceptions of Black threat across a variety of situations. In most contexts when I have been with my godchildren, their friends, or relatives, my presence has appeared to lower the likelihood of either authority figures or White civilians acting in an aggressive, confrontational manner toward the young Black persons whom I accompanied. For instance, while my godsons were confronted by security guards at the mall in Ocean County on two occasions when they were by themselves, my godsons were never harassed when I was with them at the mall. On one occasion I was with all of my godchildren and two of their friends (three Black male and three Black female teenagers) at the mall in Ocean County, and the same security guard who had confronted my godsons on a prior visit made no attempt to confront us as we all congregated briefly in this guard's vicinity. As I note in Chapter 8, my privileges and power as a White authority figure were qualified or neutralized in some settings. Nevertheless, the "threat" posed by young Black people, even in spaces that authorities appeared to mark as "White", seemed to dissipate when I or another White authority figure was seen by onlookers as having ties to the young Black persons in the situation.

Consequences of equating Blackness with threat

While the threat of Blackness has varied across contexts, the totality of the experiences I have had either directly or vicariously with young Black persons suggest that there is an overarching association of Blackness with threat in this society and conversely an association of Whiteness with safety and harmlessness. These racialized associations of threat and safety play out in a number of deleterious ways for those whom society identifies as Black. As a result of this association of Blackness with threat, Black persons do not enjoy the same freedom to move, act, and just be that White persons enjoy across spaces and contexts. Rennie summed up this feeling of limited freedom when he stated, "I can't even ride a bike without being accused of something".

This association of Blackness with threat also means that Black people are more likely to be scrutinized by and have unwanted, unwarranted encounters with authority figures. In turn, the greater likelihood of such encounters translates into a greater likelihood of problematic, life-altering outcomes. For instance, Black people are more likely to have encounters with school officials that lead to greater rates of suspension and expulsion from school than that of Whites.[87] Likewise, Black people are more likely than Whites to have encounters with law enforcement,[88] which increases the probability that Black people will become entangled in the criminal justice system and face punitive sanctions.

Racialized associations of threat and safety also increase the likelihood of deadly outcomes in two different respects. Black people's greater probability of encounters with police increases the probability that Black people will experience violent, deadly encounters.[89] White people's greater probability of avoiding police scrutiny and receiving kid-glove treatment from authorities increases the probability of some Whites' unchecked pathological behaviors metastasizing into acts of violence. For instance, the overwhelming majority of mass shootings in the US have been perpetrated by White males who have been overlooked by authorities.[90]

The potentially calamitous outcomes stemming from associations of Blackness with threat create a whole range of stressors with which Whites like me do not have to wrestle. For Black people who have to psychically manage such stressors, it suggests that navigating the social landscape in the US for many Black people is akin to walking through a minefield. The perceptions of threat that shape this minefield are exacerbated by the related, concomitant perceptions of presumed guilt, to which I now turn in Chapter 6.

Learning objective
Recognizing the variability of racial meanings

The reader will recognize how racial meanings vary by social context. The reader will be able to articulate examples of how place, time, and demographic factors such as age, gender, and social class affect the way race is perceived and understood.

- Identify examples of how racial meanings vary by place.
- Identify examples of how racial meanings vary by time.
- Identify examples of how racial meanings vary by age.
- Identify examples of how racial meanings vary by gender.
- Identify examples of how racial meanings vary by social class.

6
Presuming Black guilt

The race "lessons" I have learned about people's associations of Blackness with threat are closely related to concomitant lessons I have received about how people equate Blackness with presumptive guilt. In this chapter I explore how associations of Blackness with guilt play out in contexts inside and outside of schools, and in Chapter 7 I delve into efforts to create and protect White innocence. My godchildren's experiences and the experiences of young Black persons whom I have known through a variety of educational contexts have revealed five different scenarios in which people have equated Blackness with presumptive guilt. In providing examples of each of these scenarios below, I emphasize not only authorities' tendency to home in on alleged Black "perpetrators", but also how authorities' presumption that Black persons are guilty of some offense precludes authorities from seeing and addressing the culpability of White perpetrators.

Manufacturing guilt out of racial stereotypes

One scenario that has unambiguously revealed a presumption that Black people are guilty of some type of criminality/wrongdoing has involved situations where people, usually authority figures, manufacture guilt based on racial stereotypes. These situations where there is no discernible empirical evidence of suspicious activity that would warrant the initiation of an encounter are commonly referred to as racial profiling. The only apparent, logical explanation for such encounters is that the initiator believes that Black people generally engage in criminal and deviant activity. My godchild Rennie has had multiple encounters with police that reflect this manufacturing of guilt. For instance, after Rennie, then 18 years old, purchased a beat-up, old pickup truck from a farmer in Ocean County, he was pulled over by a White male police officer in Thornton, even though Rennie was driving the speed limit and had not otherwise violated any traffic laws. The officer ordered Rennie out of the truck, and after glancing at some remnants of hay that were in the cargo bed of the truck, began to grill Rennie about having marijuana stashed in the truck. Convinced that the hay was marijuana, the officer persisted in grilling Rennie for approximately 45 minutes about "coming clean" about this phantom marijuana and repeatedly threatened to bring out drug-sniffing dogs and prolong the encounter even further. Rennie calmly kept telling the officer that there was no marijuana in the vehicle. Seeing that these protestations were falling on deaf ears, Rennie allowed the officer to search the vehicle. The officer found nothing but hay, and some 75 minutes after pulling over Rennie, the officer finally let Rennie go without any traffic citations. The officer not only offered no apology, but actually admonished Rennie to "stay out of trouble".

Another incident Rennie experienced as a 17-year-old clearly spells out how authority figures' assumptions of guilt are selectively skewed against Black people. During the summer of 2004, Rennie was pushing an electric scooter on his way to work in Seeburg. A patrol car slowly followed Rennie for a couple of blocks and finally rolled up on Rennie as he turned down a side street. An officer in the car yelled out the window, "You got a license for that thing?" Rennie replied, "I don't need a license, it's electric". Not satisfied, the officer then said, "Let me see, turn it on". Rennie then turned the key, and said, "See". Throughout this encounter, Rennie noticed how the officer's demeanor changed from excitement (at the possibility of seizing the scooter) to disappointment. What is remarkable about this seemingly minor encounter is how racially selective it was. For over a half dozen years, Rennie had observed hundreds of young Whites riding gas-powered mopeds and motorized dirt bikes all over Seeburg, and most noticeably in a large dirt lot near Rennie's apartment, and not once had he ever seen a Seeburg police officer stop one of these White bikers and ask for proof of a license.

Starting at age 13, Rennie's friend Iggy had 3 similar encounters with police in Seeburg when walking over to the home of a friend who lived in an all-White neighborhood. On each occasion that officers stopped Iggy, they would ask Iggy where he was going, and then would search Iggy's person. During the hot summer months, Iggy carried a small, unmarked bottle of cologne to mitigate the effects of excessive sweating. Each time officers discovered the cologne bottle, they assumed that they had stumbled upon alcohol or some other illicit liquid substance and would proceed to ask Iggy a series of questions about the contents of the bottle. Even after sniffing the bottle and determining that it in fact contained cologne, the officers would nevertheless admonish Iggy about using and dealing illegal substances and would act like they were disappointed that they had not found some contraband.

Omar, a Black male undergraduate student who took several of my classes at Harper College in the early 2000s, had a number of experiences similar to those of Iggy and Rennie. On one occasion, Omar, who was on his way to work at approximately 6:30 a.m., was pulled over by a White male police officer who had followed Omar for several blocks in Shelton, New Jersey. Omar, like Rennie, had violated no traffic laws. When the officer came over to the car, Omar politely asked the officer why the officer had pulled Omar over. The officer provided no explanation, but rather began badgering Omar about having illegal drugs in the car. Omar continued to request an explanation for the stop, and the officer became increasingly belligerent, threatening to call for drug-sniffing dogs if Omar did not permit the officer to search the vehicle. About 30 minutes into the encounter, the officer finally relented and let Omar go without any traffic citations or an apology. Omar was then late for work.

Omar had another analogous experience with a campus police officer at Harper. While walking to a gym on campus to do some exercises to rehabilitate a knee injury, Omar noticed that a White campus officer appeared to be following Omar. Omar went to the gym and did a few exercises as the officer lurked nearby. Upon leaving the gym, Omar noticed that the officer was again following

Omar. After a couple of blocks, the officer stopped Omar and began to pepper him with questions about what he was doing at the gym, whether he was actually a student at the college, and if he possessed illegal drugs. Omar showed the officer his college identification (ID) card, explained that it was self-evident as to what he was doing at the gym, and demanded to know why this officer was following Omar. The officer then questioned the authenticity of Omar's college ID card and proceeded to lecture him about people coming from "the outside" and selling illegal drugs to Harper students. After approximately 20 minutes, the officer let Omar go without ever providing an explanation as to why the officer had singled out Omar.

This manufacturing of guilt by authority figures has even occurred when young Black persons have reached out to help out White civilians who have been experiencing some type of crisis. On one occasion, Rennie noticed an older White person who appeared to be in distress by the side of a road. This person's car had broken down on a day when the temperature was in the upper 90s, and the person seemed to be dehydrated and disoriented. After speaking briefly with this person, Rennie went over to a convenience store nearby and purchased a large bottle of water for the person. By the time Rennie returned with the water bottle, two White police officers were on the scene. As Rennie walked over to the car, he was immediately accosted by one of the officers, who, in a threatening tone, demanded to know why Rennie was coming over to the vehicle, and if Rennie had done something to harm this motorist. Rennie explained to the officer about purchasing a water bottle for the distressed motorist, but the officer dismissed Rennie's account and scolded

Rennie for "meddling". Rather than seeing Rennie as a "Good Samaritan", this officer perceived Rennie as a criminal who either had done something to hurt the motorist, or who had come over to the car to rob the motorist. Like in the other aforementioned incidents, the officer's apparent stereotypical assumptions about Black deviance and criminality convinced the officer that Rennie must be guilty of something.

Proactive or anticipatory assumptions of Black guilt have played out in other contexts outside of encounters with law enforcement. Keyana, a Black undergraduate student, described how her White managers and coworkers at a big box retail store that she worked at for a couple of years in Weston, New Jersey routinely grilled Black customers who were returning items but had a laissez-faire approach with White customers returning items. Keyana noted that her managers and coworkers openly talked about Black customers being "scammers" who engaged in fraud. Consistent with their view of Black customers, Keyana's managers and coworkers would insist on receipts from Black customers and often challenged the authenticity of receipts that Black customers presented. In contrast, Keyana observed many White customers who were permitted to return items without providing a receipt. Keyana's managers' and coworkers' presumptions that Black customers invariably tried to perpetrate fraud led to these managers and coworkers selectively profiling these Black customers.

When in doubt, blame a Black person

A second scenario in which Blackness has been equated with guilt involves situations where a problematic incident occurs, but neither the authorities nor civilians know who is responsible for what has happened. In these situations, despite the existence of multiple potential suspects who are White, authorities are quick to pin the blame on a Black person. An incident in which police initially blamed my godchild Coleman for throwing a projectile at a moving vehicle exemplifies this scenario. In June 2001, someone hurled a rock through the front windshield of a car on a road adjacent to the apartment complex in Seeburg where Monique, Rennie, and Coleman lived. Just before the incident occurred, Coleman, wearing a bright red work shirt, returned home from a shift at a part-time job and was conversing with a crowd of 15 or so people, all of whom were White except for Coleman, Rennie, and another Black man who lived at the complex. Two Seeburg officers showed up at the apartment complex a few minutes later, and first questioned the driver of the damaged vehicle. The driver told the police about only remembering seeing a red shirt immediately before hearing the windshield shatter. The police then walked over to the crowd of people standing outside of the complex and headed straight over to Coleman. Coleman, who is 6 feet tall, and weighed over 200 pounds at the time, stood out in the crowd both in terms of physical size and the red-colored shirt. The officers then proceeded to interrogate Coleman, asking why Coleman threw the rock and admonishing Coleman that greater punishment would result if Coleman did not confess. Coleman, Rennie, and some of the others gathered outside of the complex protested that Coleman was innocent, and that Kenny, a maladjusted 19-year-old White person who lived at the complex, was the perpetrator. The officers dismissed these protestations out of hand. Just as the officers were placing handcuffs on Coleman, Rennie found a discarded slingshot that Kenny had used, and reluctantly Kenny admitted being the perpetrator. Rather than conducting a thorough investigation, the officers in this situation were certain that they had the guilty party solely based on assumptions about people with Black skin and a vague reference to the color of a shirt.

Round up the usual suspect

A third scenario in which Blackness has been equated with guilt is where there is some indication that both Black and White people have been involved in a problematic incident in some way, but authority figures only single out and punish the Black persons. The most common type of incident reflecting this scenario has involved physical altercations between young Black and White persons. For instance, a fight that Evie observed between a Black student and a couple of White students that broke out in the bleachers of the gym at BHS during an assembly resulted in only the Black student being punished. What adds to the injustice of authorities' racially selective response to this incident, as well as all of the other similar cases with which I am familiar, is that young White persons appeared to have instigated these altercations. In every case of which I am aware, White students initiated altercations through some type of racially motivated taunting.

White students' initiation of altercations through racial taunting was most evident in what happened to Coleman throughout Coleman's tenure at BMS and the first part of his time at BHS. For several years, Coleman, who was often the only Black student in a variety of school settings, was incessantly taunted by a group of White, mostly male, students who called him n*****, made other racially offensive insults, and sometimes initiated some kind of physical contact. For instance, White students routinely chanted "N*****, n*****, n*****" on the bus, repeatedly said, "Lock your lockers, there's a n***** in here and he'll steal your stuff", and said, "I don't want that n***** on my team" when choosing teams in gym class. Coleman had to walk through an unrelenting gauntlet of "n*****" references in the halls as well as in some classrooms. In general, most teachers, administrators, and other school personnel stood by and said or did nothing. Coleman indicated that it was the norm at BMS and BHS for White students to use the epithet "n*****" and engage in racial harassment, and that teachers and administrators typically did not treat these practices as a big deal. While a minority of teachers tried to quell White students' onslaught of racial epithets and harassment, usually such responses were tepid and ineffectual at best. Without any support or help from school staff, Coleman often took matters into his own hands and fought back against these degradations, which invariably led to his suspension. With the exception of one time, none of the White students who initiated the racial taunting were suspended along with Coleman.

School authorities' racially selective punishment has been evident in how they have handled other types of incidents involving both Black and White students. For instance, Keenan, the 16-year-old Black student who attended a predominantly White high school in Bedford in Ocean County, described an incident in which school officials caught a Black student and two White students vaping under a stairwell at Bedford High School. Despite all three students being caught red-handed in the middle of the school day, school authorities only escorted the Black male student down to the office, and only the Black male student was punished for the incident.

Authorities' apparent readiness to selectively blame and punish Black students and selectively absolve or display leniency with White students suggests that these authorities' perception and cognition may be tainted by racial stereotypes. If Black students act in ways that are consonant with preexisting criminal- or deviance-related stereotypes about Blacks, this then makes these stereotypes salient and leads to a greater likelihood of punishment. For instance, if Black students get involved in a fight, this resonates with stereotypes about Blacks being pugilistic and violent, and leads to Black students like Coleman being seen as more culpable. Similarly, racial stereotypes about Blacks' illegal drug use and drug dealing are likely to be activated when Black students engage in any drug-related behavior (e.g. vaping). Conversely, authorities appear to have trouble in seeing young White persons as troublemakers, as such behavior is incongruent with racial stereotypes that authorities hold about Whites. Moreover, racial stereotypes may also predispose authorities to see Black students as the ringleaders when there is a mixed-race group. If Black students are seen as influencing White students, then White students are less likely to be viewed as culpable.

In the case of incidents involving racial taunting, like those Coleman experienced in school in Baldwin, the downplaying of race and racism in the schools and the overall "happy talk" presentation of the school environment as being colorblind likely contributes to the racially selective punishment in such incidents. If school officials are in denial of the reality that some White students engage in racially motivated taunting, then it is less likely that these officials will see these students as blameworthy. If the racial taunting is obscured, then it appears that Black students are being pugilistic for no legitimate reason. Any physical responses by Black students are then seen as flowing from their "nature" (and consistent with racial stereotypes) as opposed to stemming from Whites' hate-based aggression in those school environments.

They did what? It must be true!

A fourth scenario in which Blackness has been equated with guilt involves situations where someone has leveled accusations against a Black person, and other people credulously accept these accusations as being true without investigating their merit. Two particular cases that exemplify this scenario involved accusations of misconduct made against two Black female undergraduate students at Odawa College, a predominantly White college in New Jersey at which I taught. Although both students had never been in any kind of trouble, Odawa staff members and administrators immediately accepted the allegations as being true, when in fact they were false.[91]

The first case involved a student named Makayla, whom I got to know very well through a diversity club that I helped create and then supervised at Odawa. During Makayla's final year, one of Makayla's three roommates accused Makayla of harassment. Before Makayla was even aware of the accusation, supervisors from two of Makayla's on-campus jobs whisked Makayla into a conference room and blindsided Makayla with the roommate's allegations. In a hostile, accusatory tone, supervisors with whom Makayla had worked, gotten along, and trusted for several years, confronted and grilled Makayla, demanding that Makayla admit responsibility and explain the harassment. In condemning Makayla's alleged behavior, these supervisors, all of whom were White, also told Makayla how disappointed they were.

Within a couple of days, Makayla's roommate's allegations of harassment were quickly proven to be utter fabrications. For instance, the roommate's claim that Makayla had driven a car over some of the roommate's belongings was proven to be baseless because Makayla did not have a car. It turned out that the roommate was schizophrenic and had been making wild, unsubstantiated allegations against other people and acting erratically. Nevertheless, Odawa staff credulously believed the roommate's allegations before doing an independent investigation. Moreover, staff assumed that these allegations were true despite Makayla's stellar record as a model student. Makayla was not only an A student, but was the president of the diversity club and a multiracial sorority for three years, had been heavily involved in creating and moderating extracurricular programs, had stood up for the rights of students on campus (e.g. organizing a petition to keep the college's diversity goal in its strategic plan), and had worked at a number of jobs on campus (e.g. at the Women's Center and Student Life). The staff's credulity in this instance, and disregard of Makayla's long record of exemplary character, suggests that they harbored some deep-seated stereotypical beliefs regarding Black people's deviant "nature". These beliefs appear to have been activated once the allegations against Makayla were made, and once activated, eclipsed Makayla's extensive and consistent record of good character. Staff members acted as if Makayla had some kind of "Black deviant essence", and that once this "essence" came to light, that was all that they needed to presume that Makayla was guilty.

The second case involved a student named Halima, who came to see me during the fall of her senior year after a psychological counselor recommended that Halima speak with me about a traumatic encounter Halima had had with a White male campus safety officer.[92] This officer, Gondal, assaulted and harassed Halima during this encounter, wrote a campus safety report that led to several student conduct violations, and filed criminal assault charges against Halima. The response of Odawa staff and administrators to Gondal's allegations against Halima and later to an appeal of Halima's student conduct convictions revealed how these staff members and administrators presumed Halima was guilty despite a plethora of evidence casting doubt on the veracity of Gondal's account of the encounter.

Halima's fateful encounter began on a late October night, when she went to check on her friend Kyla, who is also Black, in the aftermath of a large party that campus security officers had shut down. Seeing that Kyla appeared to be intoxicated and in some form of distress, Halima called Kyla's boyfriend, Curt, who is Black, to come and assist Kyla. Shortly after Curt arrived to tend to Kyla, Halima began to walk back to a residence hall when she was aggressively confronted by officer Gondal. In a brash and intimidating manner, Gondal told Halima that Halima was not free to leave. When Halima asked Gondal why, Gondal repeatedly stated Halima was "a witness".[93] Gondal then proceeded to fold his arms and block Halima's path as if he were a football lineman. Halima tried to maneuver around Gondal, but Gondal violently grabbed Halima's arm. Gondal then continued to tail and verbally harass Halima, notwithstanding another campus safety officer telling Gondal to "let her go". A Marion[94] police officer then arrived on the scene, and Halima complained to this officer about Gondal's harassment. The Marion officer recommended that Halima obtain Gondal's badge number. Halima indicated not being comfortable in approaching Gondal for the badge number, and so the Marion officer asked Gondal to provide Halima with the number. At this point, nearly an hour into the encounter, Gondal first asked Halima to provide identification. Feeling traumatized and threatened by Gondal, Halima refused to comply with Gondal's request. Gondal persisted in demanding that Halima furnish identification. After several of Halima's friends came over to see what was happening, Halima reluctantly complied with Gondal's request for identification. The presence of Halima's friends and the Marion officer made Halima feel secure enough to supply the college identification card to Gondal. Gondal then backed off from Halima and allowed Halima to walk away, nearly 80 minutes after Halima had arrived to check on Kyla's welfare.

The following day, Halima learned that Gondal had filed criminal assault charges against Halima with the Marion police and had written up a campus safety report in which he alleged that both Halima and Curt physically assaulted him. Based on this report, Odawa's Office of Judicial Affairs charged Halima with four student conduct violations. Halima's Judicial Affairs hearing was held several days later, and from the beginning of the hearing, Halima felt that Malloy, the White male Judicial Affairs officer presiding over Halima's case, presumed that Halima was guilty. Malloy displayed no interest in hearing Halima's side of the story and relentlessly tried to get Halima to admit to violating campus rules. Curt was the only witness who could attend the hearing on such short notice, but Curt's testimony appeared to have no credibility with Malloy. There was no opportunity to present other student witnesses who could have corroborated Halima's testimony. For instance, David, a Black student who witnessed Gondal grab Halima's arm, did not get a chance to share these observations. There also was neither consideration of what the other campus security officer witnessed the night of the encounter, nor what the Marion officer saw that night. Aside from Gondal's report, the main "evidence" against Halima was an audio recording of the latter part of Halima's encounter with Gondal. This partial recording, which Gondal commenced about a half hour into the encounter and well **after** Gondal grabbed Halima's arm, captured Halima's initial refusal to provide identification to Gondal. Malloy saw this recording as particularly damning because Halima, who was highly agitated and traumatized at that point, used profanities several times, including the word "mother****er". Based on this "evidence", Malloy found Halima guilty of a "disorderly persons" offense and a "failure to comply" offense. Odawa then gave Halima a $300 fine, required that Halima perform 20 hours of community restitution, and placed the 2 convictions on Halima's college record.[95]

After meeting with Halima that November, I began a series of efforts to try to get the criminal charges against Halima dropped and to compel Odawa to grant Halima a new hearing and reverse the two student conduct convictions. I first advised Halima to file an affirmative action complaint against Gondal for racial harassment. Halima already had filed criminal assault charges against Gondal with the Marion police after learning of Gondal's criminal assault complaint, but the affirmative action complaint created some additional leverage to force Gondal to drop the criminal complaint. I then reached out to Odawa's Ombudsperson, who arranged a meeting between Gondal and Halima. Eventually Gondal agreed to drop his criminal complaint in exchange for Halima dropping both the criminal complaint and the affirmative action complaint.[96] In order to try to convince Odawa officials to grant Halima a new hearing and reverse Halima's student conduct convictions, I drafted a lengthy letter based on interviews with Halima and several witnesses, including David, Curt, and Kyla. After obtaining several faculty and staff signatures, I sent this letter to three administrators, all of whom were White. I also tried contacting the only Black member of Odawa's Board of Trustees.[97]

Several weeks later, I received a rather brusque letter from an administrator denying our request for a new hearing. Without addressing the numerous problematic issues that I raised about Gondal's conduct as well as the Judicial Affairs hearing, the letter dismissively indicated that the findings were appropriate and there was nothing untoward about either Gondal's or Malloy's actions. I arranged a meeting with this administrator to discuss the rejection of our appeal, and in a hostile tone, the administrator reiterated standing by the findings of Judicial Affairs and indicated that there was nothing else to investigate or discuss about the matter. The administrator specifically referenced Gondal's partial recording of the encounter with Halima as incontrovertible evidence of Halima's "belligerent" conduct that night. The administrator also effectively threatened me to not pursue the matter any further, as the administrator indicated that another administrator, who was my ultimate boss, concurred with the findings.[98]

The response of the administrators to the appeal request and the response of Malloy and the other White Judicial Affairs personnel to the allegations against Halima at the hearing both reflected a belief in the certainty of Halima's guilt notwithstanding a litany of problems with Gondal's account and Gondal's behavior on other occasions. The credulity of these staff and administrators in uncritically accepting Gondal's account at face value, and their insouciance in overlooking the many problems with that account, suggest that they presumed Halima was guilty because Halima was Black. There was no need to look any further into what transpired that October night because Halima's Blackness was all the "evidence" they needed. These staff and administrators' certainty was ratcheted up by Halima's use of profanity directed at Gondal. Halima's cursing at Gondal appeared to make her "Blackness" more salient in the minds of these staff and administrators, as it conjured up stereotypical thoughts of violent, uncivil "ghetto" Blacks.

The power of racial presumptions of guilt to obscure and corrupt judgment in this case is staggering when one considers all of the glaring red flags Odawa staff and administrators disregarded in considering Gondal's account of what had happened. The testimony of the student witnesses Curt and David,[99] as well as the other campus safety officer and the Marion officer, corroborated Halima's account and contradicted Gondal's account. Gondal conveniently did not turn the audio-recorder on until approximately a half hour **after** he had grabbed Halima's arm and had begun badgering Halima, which hid Gondal's initiation of the encounter and provocation of Halima. Gondal only first requested that Halima provide identification **after** the Marion officer gave Halima Gondal's badge number. The timing of this identification request throws into question Gondal's motives. Did Gondal seek Halima's identification because Gondal was worried that she was going to file a criminal assault complaint against him? Did Gondal use Halima's identification information to file a false campus safety report and bogus criminal assault charges as preemptive, self-protective moves that painted Halima as the aggressor? If Gondal had been assaulted by Halima, why did Gondal not mention it to the Marion officer on the scene that October night? Why was there no consideration of how the context of the encounter had shaped Halima's initial noncompliance with Gondal's identification request? Was it unreasonable for Halima to be afraid to share personal information with someone after being assaulted and threatened? How likely is it that a sober, diminutive person such as Halima, who stood at 5'5" and weighed 115 pounds, would initiate a physical assault against a 6'0" officer weighing 185 pounds? How likely is it that a quiet, shy, mild-mannered person like Halima, who had never been in a physical altercation and who had no record of any kind of misconduct, would assault an officer? Why was the provocation by Gondal not taken into account as the reason for Halima's loss of composure and use of profanity that evening? Why did Odawa administrators ignore the findings of the Affirmative Action

Officer that showed that Gondal had anger management issues and appeared to harbor animosity toward Black students? Why were Black students' prior complaints against Gondal summarily ignored?[100] All of these red flags suggest that even a superficial investigation of Gondal and the allegations in Gondal's report would have cast doubt on Gondal's motives and the veracity of Gondal's account. As I have gleaned from other "lessons" I have learned from Black young persons, this incident demonstrates how authority figures tend to highly scrutinize Black persons and sanction them harshly for any perceived transgressions, but generally give White persons a pass.

The Odawa staff and administrators' mishandling of Halima's case is analogous to how mostly White police and prosecutors have mishandled many cases involving Black defendants, such as the "Central Park Five"[101] and Vincent Simmons.[102] Police and prosecutors in these latter cases have ignored contradictory or tainted evidence and have not pursued other credible leads because they were so convinced that they had their suspect(s). Working on Halima's case not only afforded me an inside view of how assumptions about Black guilt infect and corrupt authorities' decision-making, but also provided an intimate look into how institutional actors become invested in their uncritical, racialized assumptions of guilt and go to great lengths to rationalize and cover up any discrepancies in their accounts when they are challenged.

Racialized attributions of blame

A fifth scenario in which Blackness has been equated with guilt involves situations where both Black and White persons are clearly acknowledged as having engaged in the same problematic conduct, but different attributions are proffered for their conduct. These attributions amplify the Black persons' guilt and mitigate the White persons' guilt. Two incidents in the mid-1990s involving RHS students who were arrested by authorities for illegally possessing a gun exemplify this scenario. Darius, a Black male student and star basketball player whom I had got to know through substitute teaching, was arrested off campus in the spring of 1995 on a sidewalk near Darius's home for carrying an unlicensed pistol. Gary, a White male honors student whom I had taught in 1994, was arrested in the fall of 1996 for bringing an unlicensed pistol to school.

In the wake of the revelations about Darius's arrest and suspension from school, teachers and other staff members were quick to condemn Darius's gun possession. One teacher sarcastically referred to Darius as a "wannabe gangbanger", while a guidance counselor said, "It turns out the star [basketball player] is really just a thug". In discussing Darius's gun possession, these RHS staff members framed it through a criminal lens. They presented Darius's deviant behavior as being a willful, intentional act for which Darius was solely to blame.

In contrast, when Gary's arrest and suspension for gun possession came to light, RHS teachers and other staff members took a more forgiving, understanding approach. Several teachers brought up how Gary was likely being bullied and had safety-related fears. Moreover, these teachers always prefaced their comments about Gary by indicating what a good student Gary was, how polite and respectful Gary was, and how this episode was so out of character for Gary. In discussing Gary's gun possession, RHS staff members framed it through an environmental lens. They presented Gary's deviant behavior as being due to outside environmental forces such as bullying, and in doing so, suggested that Gary was not fully to blame for bringing the gun to school.[103]

The starkly different responses of RHS staff members to Darius's and Gary's gun possession demonstrate how preconceived notions tied to race can either magnify or lessen blame for a particular behavior. While RHS members were quick to soften Gary's blameworthiness by referencing Gary's pleasant demeanor, good character, and reasonable concerns about being bullied, they played up Darius's blameworthiness by omitting the fact that Darius was a solid B student, had never been suspended from school, always was polite and respectful in class, and likely experienced some type of threat in the neighborhood that compelled him to protect himself. Even though Darius's and Gary's cases were strikingly similar in many ways,[104] attributing a criminal explanation for Darius's gun possession and an environmental explanation for Gary's gun possession was consistent with an overall pattern of presuming that young Black persons are unambiguously guilty and responsible for their actions. Unlike Gary, Darius was assumed by RHS staff to be acting in a manner consistent with a crime-prone character, and therefore Darius was unworthy of any sympathy.

Consequences of racial presumptions of guilt

Each of the five scenarios discussed in this chapter shows how assumptions of Black guilt often lead to authorities' misguided actions, and sometimes lead to unjust outcomes. As a result of such assumptions of racialized guilt, some young Black persons are forced to navigate a gauntlet of humiliating, gratuitous harassment, and others are placed in the untenable position of having to fight wrongful accusations and pronouncements. In addition, these racialized assumptions of guilt allow for White perpetrators of harmful conduct to avoid scrutiny and accountability, and to continue perpetrating such harm (as in the case of the young White males who racially taunted Coleman for years without virtually any accountability).

Learning objective
Recognizing expectations associated with Blackness and Whiteness

The reader will recognize how people often associate Blackness with low expectations when evaluating ability, behavior, and outcomes, and equate Whiteness with high expectations.

- Educators often assume what about Black people's intellectual ability?
- Educators often assume what about White people's intellectual ability?
- What assumptions do people make about Black people's behavior?
- What assumptions do people make about White people's behavior?

7
Protecting White innocence

People's efforts to proactively and reactively presume and amplify Black guilt have been matched by converse efforts to preserve and protect White innocence when White people have or may have engaged in a behavior that could be labeled as racist or otherwise problematic. I have observed a wide range of efforts, particularly in educational contexts, to create and maintain an image of Whites as blameless, law-abiding, and virtuous. Consistent with the concept of managing a discreditable stigma,[105] authority figures and other people have tried to keep Whites' problematic behavior hidden when that behavior is not yet known to others. In the first part of this chapter, I discuss some of the often elaborate, covert, subterranean efforts people have made to cover up and hide Whites' bad behavior, especially when it could be construed as racially discriminatory or harassing. Consistent with the concept of managing a discredited stigma,[106] authority figures and others have engaged in a variety of techniques to minimize any potential reputational damage when Whites' problematic behavior becomes known to others. I address several of these techniques in the balance of this chapter. These efforts generally have been successful in preventing Whites from being stigmatized as "racist" or deviant in some other way and have helped to perpetuate the myth that the US is a colorblind society.

Covering up and hiding problematic White behavior

My connections to young Black persons have afforded me the opportunity to behold the often extensive, behind-the-scenes efforts that some people have made to cover up and keep hidden White persons' problematic behavior. In general, there has been a greater sense of urgency to these covert efforts to hide behavior when such behavior could be perceived as "racist". This added urgency to protect and maintain the innocence of individual White persons who have or may have engaged in racist behavior likely stems from concerns about how such behavior could reflect badly on institutions, as well as other people affiliated with those institutions, particularly other White persons. White administrators' actions in Halima's case, discussed at length in Chapter 6, are illustrative of such efforts. Odawa administrators went to great lengths to cover up campus safety officer Gondal's assault and harassment of a Black student, and Gondal's prior history of problematic interactions with Black students. These administrators doubled down at every stage of Halima's long, painful ordeal, and seemed to be most concerned about avoiding any public scrutiny of how they handled Halima's case, as it would make them and Odawa College appear to be racially insensitive.

The elaborate efforts to which some authorities have gone to cover up Whites' behavior that might be construed as racist were on display in an incident that my godchild Evie experienced at the end of her senior year in high school in 2005. Evie was one of two Black students who went on a senior trip down to Walt Disney World, and Evie brought a small camcorder on the trip to record highlights. On the first night of the trip, a White teacher from BHS barged into the hotel room that Evie was sharing with three other students—one Black and the other two White. Evie and the three other students were under the bed when the teacher walked into the room. The teacher made a few strange, disparaging comments, and then left the room. Evie recorded the encounter on her camcorder, which the teacher appeared to notice before leaving the room, and then thought nothing more about the encounter.

On Evie's first day back at BHS after her return from the trip, Evie and Fatima, the other Black person who went on the trip, were summoned to the BHS Principal's office. Neither Evie nor Fatima had a clue as to why Principal Orrico wanted to see them. Orrico, who I found to be somewhat petulant and pugnacious in several meetings over the years, proceeded to interrogate Evie and Fatima about what they knew about a video recording that was made on the class trip. In a threatening tone, Orrico demanded to know who possessed a camcorder, who recorded scenes in the hotel, and what was on the videotape.[107] Orrico indicated that the recording might contain compromising footage of the White teacher who came into Evie's hotel room unannounced, and that this footage might violate the teacher's "privacy". Evie then claimed ownership of the camcorder and admitted briefly recording the teacher in the hotel room. Orrico then ordered Evie to retrieve the camcorder. Evie brought the camcorder back to Orrico's office, and Orrico then demanded that Evie delete the footage that contained images of the teacher. Evie deleted that footage, and then Orrico let Evie return to class.

While walking through the main office adjacent to Orrico's office, Evie was immediately confronted by a White student who was an editor of BMS's yearbook. In a friendly tone, this student mentioned hearing that Evie had recorded footage of the senior trip and asked Evie if it would be possible to borrow the footage to add to a video montage that the yearbook staff members were putting together as a supplement to the yearbook.[108] Evie then gave this student all of the remaining footage of the trip. When the video montage appeared a few weeks later, Evie noticed that none of Evie's footage from the trip was included in the montage. Evie then confronted the yearbook editor and asked what had happened to the footage and requested that the editor return the footage. The yearbook editor told Evie that the footage was missing but the editor would look into it. Evie confronted the editor a couple more times before graduating that June, but each time the editor evasively told Evie that the footage could not be found. Evie never got back any of the footage from the senior trip.

This incident is striking in two respects. First, it reveals the extraordinary lengths to which authority figures appeared to go in order to preserve and protect the innocence of a White teacher who may have made some comments that could have been construed as racist or inappropriate. While neither Evie nor the other female students remembered exactly what the teacher had said, the teacher and Principal Orrico appeared to be concerned about how the video recording might reflect badly on the teacher as well as BMS. This concern was probably heightened by a widely circulated media story at the time about a teacher who had been caught on videotape making racially insensitive remarks. The BMS teacher who entered Evie's hotel room appears to have requested that Orrico use his administrative authority to get rid of the potentially damning video. Orrico, in turn, not only forced Evie to delete the footage related to the teacher, but also appeared to surreptitiously enlist the yearbook editor as a confederate to seize and destroy all of Evie's video recordings from the trip. Orrico appeared to take great pains to make sure that there would be no evidence of the teacher's interaction with Evie that could possibly tarnish the image of this teacher and BMS.

Second, as I discuss in the subsection "Protecting White innocence by demonizing Blacks or calling attention to White victimization" below, this incident reveals how authority figures sometimes demonize Blacks as a way of shifting attention away from Whites' behavior. Although Evie had innocently recorded a teacher who had barged into Evie's hotel room, Evie was nevertheless painted as a villain by Orrico. Throughout Orrico's interrogation about the video recording, Evie felt that Orrico had treated Evie as someone who had committed a criminal offense. The focus of the incident shifted away from any potentially racist or inappropriate remarks the White BMS teacher made in the hotel room to Evie's "inappropriate" recording of a BMS teacher.[109]

In contrast to these elaborate, covert efforts to preserve and protect White innocence, some efforts to cover up and hide Whites' problematic behavior have been simpler and, in some cases, more brusque. Consistent with what I observed as a student (see Chapter 2), the school curricula I have observed in both the role of an educator and as a godparent have continued to omit and heavily sanitize Whites' violence and rapacity throughout American history. In particular, episodes in which Whites have perpetrated grievous harms against people of color are either left out of the textbooks and curricula or presented in heavily watered-down form (e.g. the Native American genocide and the enslavement of Africans). These omissions or sanitized presentations help to preserve the noble, upstanding image of Whites and legitimize Whites' position atop the social order in the United States.

Unlike the quiet, imperceptible, behind-the-scenes censorship of White pathology by textbook editors and curriculum designers, some Whites have protected White innocence through very blunt, sometimes contentious, efforts to quickly shut down discussions that in any way allude to or touch upon race and racism. Consistent with DiAngelo's (2018) concept of "White fragility", I have had numerous informal encounters with mostly White teachers, guidance counselors, administrators, and other school staff members who became uncomfortable and, at times, hostile and defensive, at the mere mentioning of anything related to race. Even cryptic allusions to race often were met with immediate efforts to shut down the conversation or steer it in another direction to some other topic. For instance, on one occasion, I was sitting in the faculty lounge at RHS with three other White teachers who began talking about a couple of students who had just joined the JROTC program at RHS. I chimed in with a comment about the disproportionate number of Black students in the JROTC program, and implied that school officials appeared to be steering Black students into the program. The other teachers then abruptly ended the conversation and began talking about a teacher's daughter's upcoming wedding.

In some instances, White people's defensiveness to any allusion to race appeared to be part of a self-serving effort to protect their own innocence. This invariably occurred in my interactions with BHS administrators and guidance counselors, all of whom were White. Whenever I went into BHS to complain about my godchildren's class placements or some other issue, guidance counselors and administrators became very defensive when my godchildren's Blackness became salient in some way. When my godchildren's race became salient, these guidance counselors and administrators thought that I was accusing them of being racially discriminatory, negligent, insensitive, or indifferent. For instance, after Evie and Rennie were advised by their respective guidance counselors to skip taking chemistry, I complained to these counselors that they appeared to hold low expectations regarding what Evie and Rennie could accomplish. These two guidance counselors then huffily tried to quickly steer the conversation away from any racial overtones by bringing up standardized test scores or some other race-neutral criteria as the justification for particular class assignments. These represented many on-the-fly efforts by White BHS staff to immediately throw shade on any inferences of racially disparate treatment of Black and White students in order to preserve an impartial and fair image.

Odawa administrators engaged in similar extemporaneous efforts to shut down or sabotage any conversations that intimated negligence or insensitivity to the concerns of Black and other students of color.[110] When several Black students shared microaggressions that they had experienced at Odawa at an event entitled "I, Too, Odawa" that I had helped to organize and moderate, two White Odawa administrators attempted to hijack the discussion by asking the students what made them decide to apply to Odawa. Ironically, in attempting to bury or obfuscate Black students' complaints, Odawa administrators confirmed the very substance of administrative neglect or indifference underlying those complaints.

Protecting White innocence through casual dismissal and rationalizations

When it has not been practicable to cover up allegations of Whites' problematic statements or behavior, White authority figures have employed a number of strategies to minimize and limit any potential reputational damage that could result from such allegations. One of these strategies has been to casually dismiss allegations of Whites' inappropriate conduct through rationalizations suggesting that the conduct is not a big deal. For instance, in the spring of 1995, Ayana, a Black tenth grader who had been the best student in my honors US history I class at RHS, came to speak to me about a disturbing incident that Ayana had experienced in an art class. Ayana explained that the art teacher, who was White, had gone on a tangential rant in class about how people in the ghetto (a poorly veiled racial code word for "Black") just wanted to have lots of babies and leech off the government and hardworking taxpayers (likely meaning "White" taxpayers). Ayana then noted how a vice principal and two teachers, all of whom were White, defended the art teacher and suggested that

Ayana was "overreacting" to the teacher's comments. Despite Ayana clearly being highly distraught about this incident, the RHS staff members appeared to be trying to gaslight Ayanna into doubting that what had transpired in the art class was of any consequence.

In some cases, school officials' minimization of specific White persons' problematic behavior has occurred more implicitly. For instance, BMS and BHS officials' general failure to punish any White male students who taunted Coleman and other Black male students with racial slurs suggests that these officials did not view such racial taunting as having much import. As Evie has noted, BMS and BHS school officials did not view calling someone a n***** as being a problem; BMS and BHS officials only seemed to view Black students' physical response to such epithets as being significant.

Educators also have tried to preserve and protect White innocence on a broader level by rationalizing Whites' behavior toward people of color throughout American history. Jared, a Black student who attended high school in Marion, indicated that when slavery in the US was addressed for the first and only time in his 11th grade history class, the teacher focused on how slavery was "not that bad". Jared noted that the teacher argued that most slaveholders only owned one slave, and that slaveholders generally treated their slaves humanely. In a similar vein, Keyana, a Black female student at Harper College, indicated that a community college instructor minimized the significance of slavery by quickly rushing through a 20-minute presentation on it. Keyana said that the instructor told the class, "We don't need to spend much time on this", suggesting that other topics were more important and worthy of extended coverage.

In addition, educators have appeared to take great pains to defend White Americans' innocence when Black students openly have confronted their curricular decisions. For instance, when Jared asked his history teacher why they spent a year discussing the Nazi Holocaust but did not address other examples of genocide, particularly the Native American genocide perpetrated by European Americans, the teacher soft-pedaled the Native American genocide by playing up the horrors of the Nazi Holocaust. Jared's teacher emphasized the calculated evil of the Nazis' methods and objectives and how learning about the Nazi Holocaust was important to avoid repeating the mistakes of the past. This evasive response not only conveyed to students that the harms perpetrated against Native Americans were not as significant as those perpetrated on Jews and other victims of the Nazi Holocaust, but it reinforced the idea that the worst atrocities have been committed by people in other countries, not by White Americans in the US.

Similarly, two White RHS teachers defensively rationalized their decision to take ninth graders on a class trip to Ellis Island after Ayana and two other Black students questioned the teachers' rationales for the trip. The teachers had told students that Ellis Island had been the main destination when people immigrated to the US Ayana then commented, "My people didn't come to the US". Anita, another Black student said, "We didn't come through here; I don't know why we have to see this". Rather than using this as a teachable moment to address involuntary immigration, both RHS teachers emphasized how all students could learn something important about "our" history, the sacrifices people made in coming to the US, and how the US welcomed needy immigrants with open arms. By skirting around the issue of involuntary immigration and playing up the importance of learning about voluntary immigration, these teachers were able to help preserve an image of White Americans as generally beneficent.

Protecting White innocence by demonizing Blacks or calling attention to White victimization

Another common strategy for protecting White innocence in the wake of revelations of White malfeasance has been deflecting attention away from such malfeasance by either demonizing Blacks or calling attention to how Whites have been victimized. The demonization of Blacks often has involved turning Black victims into perpetrators.[111] For instance, when Ayana, Anita, and several other Black RHS students told the teacher chaperones that they were not interested in seeing the exhibits at Ellis Island because these exhibits could not teach them anything about their history, the teachers switched the focus away from these students feeling slighted by the teachers' dismissive responses to the students' complaints to the uncooperative and unruly behavior of Black students on the trip. Similarly, when Halima and I questioned the administration's handling of officer Gondal's abusive encounter with Halima, the administrators switched the focus away from Gondal's repugnant behavior to Halima's profane language on the audiotape. Likewise, BHS officials shifted attention away from the White male students who called Coleman a "n*****" to Coleman's uncontrollable temper and assaults on the White students. In all of these instances, not only was the spotlight turned away from Whites' alleged bad behaviors to Blacks' alleged bad behaviors, but the legitimacy of Blacks' claims of victimization by Whites was undermined. If Black students were behaving badly in some way, then this behavior casts doubt over the merit or credibility of Blacks' claims of being treated inappropriately by Whites.[112]

The most egregious example of protecting White innocence by demonizing Black victims involved a hate crime that Coleman experienced when Coleman was 18 years old. Coleman was walking with Rennie down a street in Seeburg on their way to the apartment where they lived with their mother. On the way home, Coleman and Rennie passed by a house where two White teenagers, both 15 years old, were sitting on a stone wall in front of a small house. As they had done on prior occasions, the two White teenagers yelled "n*****" at Coleman and Rennie. However, unlike on prior occasions, one of the teens spit on Coleman, who then turned to the teenager and said, "What the f***?" Having had enough of these two teenagers' racist taunts, Coleman called the Seeburg police department to report a hate crime. Coleman also called his friend Jana, who is White. The Seeburg officer, a young White male, showed up about ten minutes later, and Jana also arrived on the scene. An older brother of one of the teenagers also came outside at this point.

From the get-go, the Seeburg officer did not seem at all interested in investigating whether a hate crime had transpired. The officer did not ask the two teenagers or Coleman any questions but rather engaged in friendly banter with the older brother. After approximately 20 minutes of inaction by this officer, Coleman turned his back and started to walk away from the scene. Coleman muttered to Jana, "This is why I don't call the police". Suddenly, the Seeburg officer swooped down on Coleman from behind, handcuffed Coleman, and arrested Coleman for "disorderly conduct". The officer then took Coleman down to a holding cell at the Seeburg Police Department. After putting out a call to a family friend who was a police captain at another department in Ocean County, Coleman was finally released in the early hours of the next morning and the charges were dropped.

The Seeburg officer's actions in this case are a telling example of how even the most heinous, morally reprehensible acts by White persons can be obscured or even negated by turning Black victims of those acts into perpetrators. Even though Coleman unambiguously was a victim of a hate crime in this instance, the Seeburg officer's arrest of Coleman switched the focus from the teenage females' spitting and epithet hurling to Coleman's unruly behavior in the presence of a police officer. Moreover, not only did the officer's arrest of Coleman help to protect the White innocence of the female teenagers, but it also helped to protect the officer's own innocence. Rather than asking why this White officer did not take a hate crime seriously and lift a finger to investigate it, people would ask why Coleman had been disrespectful to this officer and noncompliant.

Instead of demonizing Black victims, some White authority figures have tried to protect White innocence by shifting attention away from Black victims to White victims. For instance, when several Black students spoke about White students calling them racial epithets, spitting at them, and otherwise mistreating them at a campus-wide forum on the state of Odawa College, an official defensively responded by saying how conservative (White) professors on campus had told this official that they did not feel that they could freely express their views on campus. By shifting the narrative to White victims, this discursive move helps to minimize the significance of Black victims' complaints and, in turn, protects White innocence.

Consequences of protecting White innocence

The combination of focusing on Black threat (see Chapter 5), presuming Black guilt (see Chapter 6), and erasing, hiding, obscuring, or minimizing White malfeasance helps to reinforce racial stereotypes beyond the school context. In turn, by reinforcing stereotypes that equate "Blackness" with "deviance" and "Whiteness" with "goodness", all of these countless incidents, even seemingly minor ones, ultimately help to replicate and sustain racial hierarchy within the US. Moreover, the extensive, varied efforts to preserve and protect White innocence make Blacks' anger and complaints appear to be illegitimate because the sources of that anger and those complaints have been hidden, neutralized, or severely minimized through those efforts. Ironically, hiding or minimizing Whites' bad behavior paves the way for Whites to claim that **they** are somehow victimized by Blacks' complaints about racism. It makes it possible for Whites to claim that Blacks' complaints are unfounded and gratuitously malign innocent Whites and innocent American institutions.[113]

8
Reflections on race privilege, power, and treatment

The countless hours that I have spent with my godchildren and other young Black persons, especially outside of formal contexts, have made me more cognizant of privileges[114] and power associated with race, more observant of how people view and treat mixed-race groups in different social contexts, and more sensitized to impediments to positive cross-racial interactions. In the first part of this chapter, I reflect on how the "race lessons" I have learned through my wide-ranging experiences with young Black persons have shaped my awareness of the privileges and power that I and other White people possess solely by virtue of being designated as "White". I also examine the situational factors that lessen or nullify such privilege and power. The second part of this chapter focuses on how others have perceived and treated me when I have interacted with Black people in different social contexts, and what these experiences reveal more broadly about how people view Black–White mixed-race groups. In the last part of the chapter, I discuss some of the factors that seem to promote healthier, more meaningful interactions between White people and Black people.

Reflections on privileges related to ability, competence, threat, and guilt

Unlike many of the young Black people I have known, I have had the privilege of being treated by others as having academic potential when I was younger, and being presumed as competent as I became older. Beginning in kindergarten, teachers assumed that I had ability and encouraged and nurtured it. Years after my family moved out of Longwood, my mother recounted that my kindergarten teacher, who was White, said that it was good that we were moving to another town because I was a "bright" boy and the Longwood elementary school was not "good enough" for me. My kindergarten teacher's lofty expectations regarding my ability are striking because unlike a couple of my Black classmates, Greg and Tamika, I could not yet read at the end of that first year of school. Clearly, I was no more precocious than these classmates were. Yet, my teacher seemed to be suggesting that the school's overwhelming Black student population was not sophisticated enough and would stultify my development, and/or that teachers at this lower-income, predominantly Black elementary school did not care enough to provide an enriching educational experience.

Up through the end of high school I encountered multiple teachers who similarly held high expectations for me and helped build my confidence and belief in myself.[115] As early as elementary school, teachers communicated to me that not only did they expect me to go to college someday but expected that I would go to a "good" college. As I noted in Chapter 4, my experience stands in stark contrast to that of my godsons, who were never encouraged to go to college by any of their teachers. In addition, unlike my godchildren and other young Black persons I have known, no educators ever suggested that I should consider going to vocational school, joining the military, or getting a job right after high school as an alternative to college.[116]

Conversely, I have enjoyed the privilege of not having to worry about being labeled as having lesser ability, and of not having to prove that I was more capable. Unlike Rennie, Iggy, Jared, and other bright young people I have known, I have not had to psychically wrestle with crushing self-doubt about my ability as a result of being designated as a "special education" student with lower ability. Moreover, unlike Rennie, Iggy, Jared, and other young Black persons, I have not had to fight tooth and nail to convince educators that my ability was greater than what they assumed or have had to deal with educators' patronizing rationalizations (e.g. "it would be too challenging for you") for placing and keeping students in special education or other low ability tracks. In addition, unlike my godchildren, I have had the privilege of not having family background factors detrimentally affect assumptions about my ability. For instance, even though my family had little money when we lived in Longwood, this lower income status did not cause my teacher to assume that I had lesser academic potential.

As I grew older, I have enjoyed the privilege of being seen as competent by others across a wide range of social situations. I have been seen as competent when I walk into a classroom to teach. I have not had to worry about people taking me seriously or questioning whether I am qualified to be in that role.[117] This stands in marked contrast to the experience of my goddaughter Monique and other young Black persons who have discussed feeling the need to work twice as hard as their White peers and colleagues in the workplace or in the classroom to be seen as competent. Moreover, unlike my goddaughter and other young Black persons, I have not had to spend time and psychic energy worrying about my presentation of self—clothes I wear and my hairstyle—in order to be taken seriously and seen as competent. I can dress casually and still be presumed to be competent.[118] I can use slang, or even some profanity, and it does not undercut or throw into question my competence.

I also have had the privilege of being viewed as competent even when I am, in fact, not. For instance, on a few occasions I have been selectively approached by other White people who have asked me, and not my Black companions, for directions.[119] On some of these occasions, I lacked knowledge of the area to be able to advise these directions-seekers, but at least one of my Black companions knew the area and was able to provide directions.

In addition to having the privilege of being perceived as having ability, I generally have also enjoyed being out in the world without being perceived as a threat,[120] and without worrying about how my appearance and behaviors might increase the likelihood that onlookers will perceive me as a potential threat. In contrast to the young Black persons, especially young Black male persons, I have known, I have not had to worry about being scrutinized when I am out in public. I have been able to move about the world freely without constantly worrying about how others may perceive and react to me.

Moreover, I have not had to expend lots of time and psychic energy preparing how to present myself before I go out into the social world. My discussions with and observations of young Black persons have made clear the numerous things that I, as a White person, have taken for granted in terms of how I present and carry myself when interacting with others in various contexts. Unlike these Black persons, I have not had to think about how my tone of voice, degree of loudness, or even voicing of an opinion might be perceived as threatening by others. I have not had to be mindful of how my demeanor, posture, or expression of emotions (e.g. showing upset) might be seen as threatening. I have, for instance, been able to argue and express anger without being seen as highly threatening. As alluded to in Chapter 4, my godsons and other young Black males have pointed out that even when they are calm, they are nevertheless perceived by some Whites as being angry and threatening. These young Black males, such as Shane, a Harper College student, have noted that even slight movements of their bodies might be misinterpreted as aggressive and threatening. Consequently, these young Black males have indicated that they need to constantly engage in self-policing of their bodies and facial expressions and have to constantly suppress natural emotional reactions to phenomena through disciplined self-restraint. I, as a White person, have not had to engage in this psychically taxing self-vigilance and dehumanizing self-policing of natural human impulses and reactions.

Unlike the young Black persons whom I have known, I also have had the freedom to engage in a whole range of other seemingly benign behaviors without considering how such behaviors might make me appear to be a threat to others. While my godsons and other Black males have noted that they think about how the clothes that they wear could possibly make them appear threatening to some onlookers in certain places, I never have engaged in such calculus. For instance, while my godsons and other Black males have reported that they sometimes have refrained from wearing hooded sweatshirts ("hoodies"), hats, jeans, and sneakers in some settings, I have never hesitated in wearing such clothing items in the same types of settings. Similarly, during the 2020s pandemic, both young Black males and females indicated that they sometimes felt nervous about wearing a mask in certain places because they feared it would cause some people to view them with increased suspicion, whereas I always wore a mask into every establishment without thinking twice about it.

Besides clothing choices and adjustments to the way they speak (e.g. avoiding slang and profanity), their tone of voice (e.g. speaking softly), and their demeanor (e.g. smiling), young Black persons have engaged in a variety of other behaviors to put others—usually White people—at ease, and to make others see their presence as innocuous and legitimate. For instance, some young Black persons have indicated that they sometimes try to put others at ease by splitting up a larger all-Black group into smaller groups so as draw less attention. I cannot remember any time I have made the same consideration about a group of which I was a part. Young Black persons also have discussed periodically engaging in practices to preemptively dispel others' perceptions that they are at a place or in an area for some illegitimate or nefarious purpose. In particular, Rennie, Coleman, and other young Black males have described certain proactive practices they undertake to minimize potential suspicion from police officers. For instance, when Rennie is confronted with a police officer on foot or in a patrol car, Rennie sometimes goes into a convenience store and buys a pack of gum to communicate to the officers that there is a legitimate reason for Rennie being in that area.[121]

Young Black persons I have known also have discussed how they think about what they need to have in their possession in the event that they are stopped by police, or if civilians question the legitimacy of their presence. For instance, Maurice, a Black undergraduate student at Harper College, always makes sure to have his driver's license and other necessary credentials when leaving home, even if Maurice is just briefly taking care of something like moving a car to comply with alternate side parking rules. Similarly, young Black persons have discussed how they are self-vigilant regarding carrying documents that convey their proof of ownership of things. For example, after purchasing a high-quality mountain bike, Rennie made sure to always carry a receipt confirming ownership of the bike in the event that police or civilians accused Rennie of stealing the bike. In contrast to these ways in which young Black persons have conditioned themselves to be self-vigilant, I have had a carefree peace of mind to leave my apartment or home without thinking about whether I have identification cards or proof of ownership with me. When I have needed to quickly move and repark my car, I invariably have done so without even thinking about bringing my driver's license with me. When I have hopped on my bike, I have never entertained the possibility that someone will question whether the bike belongs to me.

Unlike young Black persons I have known, I also have had the privilege of knowing that if some crime or other problematic event occurs, I will not automatically become a suspect. Unlike Coleman, Rennie, Jared, and other young Black persons, I have not had to worry about being stopped because I "fit the description" of a suspect.[122] In addition, I have not had to worry that I will be presumed guilty if someone makes an accusation. I have been able to rest assured that people will be open to hearing my side of the story rather than rushing to judgment.

Reflecting on the vast array of unearned privileges that have been bestowed upon me as a White person in this society has sensitized me to how much easier and less stressful life is for me and other White people compared to Black people in general. In particular, I have become mindful of the significant amount of time and psychic energy that Black people feel compelled to waste doing things to minimize or counter perceptions of threat and guilt, or to convince others of their competence. All of the privileges that I have gratuitously enjoyed as a White person also have brought into stark relief how working hard, following the rules, and becoming educated and successful do not immunize Black people from being perceived in negative stereotypical ways. Regardless of Black people's accomplishments, some may still question their competence, view them as threats, and presume that they are guilty of some transgression.

Reflections on power to affect outcomes and the limits on such power

In addition to making me more attuned to all of the aforementioned privileges I enjoy as a White person, my connections to young Black persons also have highlighted how my Whiteness has provided me with power to affect outcomes in certain circumstances. In some instances, I have had the power to serve as a quasi-escort for young Black persons in certain predominantly "White" spaces and have been able to quell authorities' threat perceptions of my Black companions in these spaces. This ability to legitimize the presence of young Black persons who have accompanied me was evident at the mall in Ocean County. As I noted in Chapter 5, security guards approached my godsons when they briefly congregated with some of their other Black friends in this mall on two separate occasions. However, on those occasions when I was with my godsons, goddaughters, and some of their other Black friends, we were not approached by any security guards. I appeared to represent an informal social control agent to these security officers, such that I allayed their fears that the Black teenagers who were with me would get out of hand in any way.

Besides having the power to function as an escort and neutralize or reduce authorities' fears of Black companions, at other times I have had the power to defuse and shut down situations with young Black persons and authority figures that otherwise could have escalated. For instance, when two fifth-grade Black boys started shoving each other after a hard foul in a pickup basketball game on the playground in Longwood in the after-school program in 2010, I was able to convince a school security guard who came over to the playground that everything was under control and there was no need to take the students down to the principal's office. Similarly, on one occasion when I was with Monique, Rennie, and Coleman on the boardwalk in Plainton in 2003, I was able to quickly shut down an encounter with a police officer who inquired about a disturbance that had occurred near us. Likewise, when Chante and Tamika's cousin Jamil ran into the middle of an outdoor dance group and disrupted their routine, I was able to convince the group's coordinator to not call the police. These instances where I have been able to defuse and shut down encounters with authority figures may again be due to these figures perceiving me as an informal social control agent. In addition, these authority figures may have viewed me as credible because of my status as a White adult.

In other cases, I have had the power to either obtain favorable outcomes for young Black persons by influencing authorities' decision-making, or by compelling these authorities to reverse their prior decisions. As I alluded to in Chapter 5, my ability to convince Newbury police to release Gladys's sons from custody after they had been arrested for vandalism is an example of the former. Appearing to these police as a White "authority" figure, I was able to convince them that Gladys's sons were not "gang" members and would not pose a threat to the community if they were released.

One notable example of my ability to influence authorities' decision-making involved my ability to convince a judge to spare Raquan, the nephew of Monique, Rennie, and Coleman, from spending any time in prison. Raquan had been with a group of adolescents who had beaten up another adolescent. Although Raquan had not been involved in the beating, Raquan was nevertheless charged with assault and was looking at possibly four years in prison. After writing a long letter attesting to Raquan's character and gentle nature, I spoke over the phone with the judge for nearly 50 minutes about Raquan.[123] Based on my recommendations, the judge sentenced Raquan to probation and a job training program.

The majority of instances where I have been able to compel authorities to reverse their prior decisions involved school authorities' decisions relating to my godchildren's schooling. For instance, toward the end of Coleman's senior year of high school, BMS Principal Orrico informed Coleman's mother, Deanna, that Coleman was not going to graduate because Coleman had missed too many days of school.[124] As a result of all of these absences, Coleman also would have to finish schooling in an alternative program and obtain a GED, because Coleman was 20 years old and had reached the maximum age at which students were permitted to attend school in the district. After Deanna unsuccessfully lobbied to prevent Coleman from being dismissed from BMS, I went in to speak with Orrico. After a rather combative meeting, I was able to convince Orrico to allow Coleman to graduate on the condition that Coleman did not miss any more days of school.[125]

My power to compel reversals of school authorities' decisions was most evident in matters related to my godchildren's class placement and curricular program. My meetings with child study members finally convinced them to take Rennie out of special education classes, and my meetings with guidance counselors resulted in Monique dropping the vocational cosmetology program, Evie being moved into College Prep English, and Rennie and Evie being placed in chemistry classes. My power as a White person became highly self-evident in these instances because the guidance counselors and child study team members had not seemed to listen to my godchildren's Black parents and grandparents prior to my interventions. These guidance counselors and child study team members seemed somewhat intimidated by my presence and shocked that someone would challenge their decision-making. Strangely enough, it was I, a White person, who made race more salient for these guidance counselors and child study team members. In doing so, I made these school personnel uncomfortable enough to agree to change their decisions (and end the discomfort of possibly being seen as racist).

While my many varied experiences with young Black persons have made me more cognizant of the power and privileges I sometimes wield based on my Whiteness, some of these experiences have also made me aware of the limits on such power and privilege. A number of experiences have shown that I do not always possess power to function as an "escort" when I am with Black people. In particular, I have not been able to minimize authorities' threat perceptions regarding my Black companions when my status as a White authority figure has been less salient. For instance, when authority figures told me and my godchildren and their nieces and nephews that we needed to disperse from the basketball court in Mansfield in 2006 (see Chapter 5), I was not seen as a White authority figure due to the fact that I dressed like a young person and was playing basketball with them.

In other instances, how authority figures or White civilians perceive my being with Black persons has precluded me from having any power in those situations to legitimize the presence of either my Black companions or myself. In some places, like some of the restaurants I discuss in the next section, the White workers and patrons have appeared to highly resent having any Black persons in these places. Rather than seeing me as a White authority figure, these White workers and patrons have seen me a "race traitor". In other places, I have lacked power because authority figures or White civilians have seen my connection to my Black companions as being deviant. In some situations, like the incident I describe with Glenda and Jamila in the next section, onlookers' assumptions that Black and White people being together is tied to some perverted or illicit purpose nullifies any power I might otherwise wield. In other situations, such as the incidents I describe at Penn Station and on I-95 in the next section, authority figures' assumptions that I, a White adult male, have contravened racial norms, not only has stripped me of any power in those situations, but also has made me seen as a "threat".

My power as a White person to affect outcomes also has been limited in certain contexts. In particular, when I have tried to challenge certain institutional decisions involving young Black persons, I have had no power where these challenges were perceived by institutional actors as threatening their own interests as well as the overall interests and reputation of the institution. This was most evident in my experience in challenging how Halima was treated by institutional actors at Odawa (see Chapter 6). Unlike Halima's situation, the situation involving the judge's sentencing of Raquan, and the situation involving Principal Orrico's decision to allow Coleman an opportunity to graduate, did not threaten those respective authority figures or the institutions they represented. The lack of power I possessed in Halima's case speaks to the power of institutionalized racism. Regardless of race, anyone who challenges such institutionalized racism is likely to seen and treated as a threat.

Reflections on how I am treated when interacting with Black people

My experiences with young Black people have made me more attentive to how race shapes how I and other people in Black–White mixed-race groups are perceived and treated across in social situations. Throughout my entire life, when I have interacted with other people recognized as "White", those around me—both White people and people of color—have not batted an eye. No one has given me strange looks or said anything to me because I was with other White people. If I have been in public with other White people's children, onlookers have unquestionably assumed that those White children were **my** children. For instance, when Zack, the son of Kurt, my cousin, wandered off to another part of a large restaurant and sat near a group of White people, the other White people in the restaurant appeared to automatically assume that Zack was my child.

In contrast, people often have taken notice of when I have interacted with Black people, and sometimes have expressed confusion or discomfort with these cross-racial interactions. I have often experienced stares when I am publicly interacting with Black people, and at times have been met with looks of disapproval or disgust, expressions of hostility and resentment, and, on a few occasions, derogatory comments and epithets. My interactions with Black persons appear to have contravened onlookers' expectations of same-race interactions to which they are accustomed. However, others' responses to my interactions with Black persons have not been uniform across social situations. Rather, how people have treated me and my Black companions has varied based on the age, sex, and perceived social class of my companions, the racial marking of spaces (e.g. if the space was seen as a "White" space), the demographic makeup of the place at the time, and what we were doing in those places.

My interactions with my godchildren and other Black children in spaces outside of formal educational contexts generally have elicited more scrutiny and curiosity from onlookers than my interactions with Black adults. When I have interacted with Black children in public spaces, I often have noticed people, especially White people, gazing at us. This gazing has been most pronounced in predominantly White spaces and communities where it is unusual to see Black people, let alone a White person interacting with Black people. While most gazes have harmlessly conveyed a sense that White onlookers saw my interactions with young Black persons as "odd" or "curious", occasionally these gazes have conveyed disapproval or disgust at our presence. For instance, in 1999, the middle-aged, White host at a restaurant located in a predominantly White shore resort town in South Jersey nonverbally conveyed displeasure when I brought Monique, Rennie, and Coleman to that restaurant for breakfast.

This host, who had smiled and taken part in friendly banter with a couple of all-White groups of patrons before seating us, engaged in eye-rolling after spotting us and continued to frown while walking away after seating us. Outside of my godchildren, there were no people of color inside the crowded restaurant at the time, and the host appeared to be nonverbally communicating to me, "Why did you bring **them** here".

White employees' disapproval of my bringing Black children to restaurants has been communicated more subtly by seating and service practices. On multiple occasions, White hosts seated all-White parties before they seated me and the Black children who were with me. I also noticed on many occasions that we were seated in the corner of a restaurant, in a spot that was less visible than other tables in the restaurant. It was as if the hosts were trying to hide our presence from the White patrons at these restaurants. Once seated, we sometimes received service after all-White parties who had been seated after us.

Whites' adverse reactions to me and my godchildren and other Black children who were out with me appeared to be greater when the children wore clothes that were associated with "Black" fashion styles, such as hip-hop styles, and when the children had certain hairstyles, particularly dreadlocks and cornrows. These clothing styles and hairstyles likely triggered more reproachful responses from some Whites because these styles made the children's "Blackness"—and their seeming difference from Whites—more salient. When the children wore more conservative-looking clothing and sported hairstyles that drew less attention (e.g. close-cropped Afros or straightened hair),

Whites were much less likely to nonverbally disapprove of our presence.

Most verbal responses either questioning or commenting on my interactions with young Black persons outside of educational contexts largely have been innocent. For instance, there were multiple occasions, particularly at parks and museums, where younger White children asked either me or my godchildren whether I was their father. As mentioned in Chapter 5, more hostile verbal responses typically have been either indirect or from a distance. For instance, the White father who yanked his son away from Monique and Rennie when they were building a sandcastle together did not directly speak to or make eye contact with either me, Monique, or Rennie. Rather, this man indirectly conveyed his disapproval by yelling at his son, "I don't want you playing with them". As previously noted, those who hurled racial epithets in three different almost exclusively White, politically conservative towns by the Jersey Shore always did so at a distance. Some yelled "n*****" and other epithets either from a moving vehicle at least 40 feet or more away, whereas others yelled these epithets when I was driving past them, again, usually from a distance of at least 30 to 40 feet.

Some Whites have communicated disapproval to the presence of me and Black children in predominantly White spaces more directly and confrontationally through disproportionately hostile, incensed responses to trivial "offenses" that the children and I have committed in their presence. On one occasion on the beach in the predominantly White town of Oceanside, New Jersey in the early 2000s, a middle-aged White person sitting in a beach chair started apoplectically berating me when a Frisbee

I was tossing with Rennie landed near this person. Similarly, in the early 2000s, the middle-aged White owner of a motel in the predominantly White town of Calvert, New Jersey became unhinged when my godchildren and I started tossing around an inflated beach ball in the motel's pool. The excessive reactions to minor transgressions in these instances suggest that these White persons likely were really upset that I had brought Black children into spaces that were typically only occupied by White people.

While my young Black companions and I often felt scrutinized, and sometimes encountered unwelcoming or hostile responses from some Whites in predominantly "White" spaces, we generally experienced little to no such scrutiny or unwelcoming treatment in racially mixed suburban settings and large, racially diverse cities. We particularly felt accepted and at ease in a handful of politically liberal, racially diverse towns in Maryland and New Jersey where it was normal to see some interracial couples and families. In these latter towns, people were generally friendly and sometimes helpful. We encountered far more people who smiled and made pleasant small talk in these towns compared to what we experienced in predominantly White towns. We also were less conscious of our cross-racial status in these racially mixed communities. In predominantly White towns, the common gaze of White people made us more conscious of our cross-racial status and made us feel that we were violating a social norm simply by being together out in the world. In contrast, there was a liberating feeling in these racially mixed communities, where we could freely be ourselves and become fully absorbed in whatever we were doing.

In general, my interactions with Black children also have been more accepted in predominantly Black communities and spaces. While Black people in these spaces appeared to notice me and the children more than in the racially mixed communities and big cities, and we sometimes encountered quizzical looks or comments regarding the status of our relationship, Black people generally were amenable my involvement with the children. This general openness to and acceptance of my involvement with the children in part might be attributable to a common view in these communities that child-rearing "takes a village". In this sense, my presence was normalized by the idea that I was simply a member of the village who was helping to raise the children. I also believe that Black people's generally positive view of my involvement with the children was due to their assessment of the children when they were with me. Unlike the White people in predominantly White settings, the Black people in predominantly Black settings were far more attentive to the children's behavior and how they appeared to get along with me. For these Black people, if the children appeared to be happy and highly comfortable with me, then I was deemed as "okay".

While the majority of Black people appeared to have no issue with my involvement with Black children, there were some Black people who, at least initially, did not approve of it. In particular, Monique, Rennie, and Coleman's older brother, father, and paternal grandmother and step-grandfather were not accepting of my relationship with my godchildren. My godchildren's older brother and father, whom neither I nor the children saw until five years after my relationship with the children had begun, resented my involvement with the children, but communicated this to me indirectly through the children. The children's brother, father, and paternal grandparents also viewed me with suspicion. They questioned my motives for being with the children and raised concerns that I might be a child molester behind my back. My godchildren's brother's and father's resentment appeared to stem from how I made them feel about themselves. My taking the children out and bringing some happiness into their often difficult lives brought into stark relief how uninvolved the brother and father were in the children's lives. The suspicions that I might be a child molester seemed to stem from the difficulty these relatives had in processing a cross-racial relationship that was outside of the realm of their experience. Moreover, both the resentment and suspicions of these relatives also likely derived from the negative experiences that these relatives generally had had with Whites over the course of their lives. My involvement with the children not only triggered thoughts of these prior negative experiences but also made it hard for them to imagine that interactions with White people could result in any kind of positive outcomes.

How I have been treated and perceived when I have been out in the world with my godchildren and other Black children also has been shaped by what the children and I were doing, irrespective of the racial makeup of spaces. When the children and I actively engaged in some activity, such that the purpose of why we were together was clear, people were far less likely to scrutinize us or view our being together as "odd". For instance, when I engaged in activities with the children at a playground, park, or museum, people were less likely to scrutinize and question why we were together. By engaging in some socially recognized purpose and demonstrating that we had some type of relationship, we were granted conditional acceptance despite our relationship being outside of the norm.

However, when I have been with the children in spaces where it was not clear as to what our purpose was in being together and what the nature of our relationship was, I have been viewed with suspicion. For instance, when I took Monique and Rennie to see a play in New York City right after their 16th birthday, I was viewed with suspicion by a police officer who saw me standing with Monique outside of the men's restroom at Penn Station. While Monique and I were waiting for Rennie, who had gone into the restroom, this officer walked up to Monique and asked her, "Are you alright?", while glancing distrustfully at me and then back at her. Similarly, when I was driving with Monique and Rennie on I-95 through Baltimore when they were 12 years old, I was pulled over by two Maryland State Troopers.[126] After pulling us over, one of the troopers walked around and peered into my car and silently mouthed to the children, "Are you okay?", while the other trooper grilled me about what we doing and where I was going. In both these incidents, my being with Black children was viewed as suspect because there was not a clear, readily evident reason as to why we were together. Moreover, the fact that these spaces were transportation-related, coupled with the infrequency of seeing White men with Black children or adolescents in this society, likely raised the specter of kidnapping or human trafficking in the minds of these officers.[127] These latter suspicions tie into much broader White supremacist-derived ideas that associate cross-racial connections as being deviant and dirty in some way and cause people to infer nefarious motives when they see cross-racial dyads, triads, or other small groups.

In comparison to people's views and responses to my interactions with Black children, people's perceptions of and reactions to my interactions with Black adults have largely depended on the sex of the Black adults. In general, my interactions with adult Black males have elicited virtually no reaction from people of all races. My interactions with Black males have been met with some stares and sideways glances on a few occasions in predominantly White spaces, but typically White onlookers perceive my adult Black male companions as "okay" in these spaces because I, a White male, have implicitly "vetted" them. In contrast, my interactions with Black adult females have often generated scrutiny and, on some occasions, have been met with disapproval and/or suggestions that such interactions were inappropriate.

The substantially greater scrutiny of my interactions with adult Black females has been most evident in predominantly "White" spaces such as restaurants in predominantly White communities. On one occasion, a Black female former undergraduate student and I instantly received stares from all of the patrons and employees of a pizza restaurant located in a predominantly White town in Middlesex County as soon as we walked into the establishment. The stares persisted for most of the time that we were seated in the restaurant. On another occasion, two older White female patrons at a restaurant in a nearly all-White community in Monmouth County rolled their eyes and gave me open looks of disgust as I ate dinner with a Black female friend.

On other occasions, I and my Black adult female companion(s) have been met by responses that suggested my association with these Black females was deviant. The most disturbing such response that my Black adult female companions and I encountered took place in a parking lot in a predominantly White shore town in Monmouth County in June 1987 when I was 21 years old. On this occasion I was with my friend Glenda, Glenda's best friend Jamila, and her coworker, George. Like Glenda, Jamila and George both were Black. We stopped at a convenience store, and Glenda, Jamila, and I waited in the car while George ran into the store. While we were waiting for George, two bearded, scraggly looking White adult males pulled up adjacent to us in a pickup truck. The White male in the passenger seat then turned to me through the open window and asked me, "Where did you pick up those hoes?" Caught off guard, as well as concerned about everyone's safety, I did not engage with these two somewhat menacing men. This incident clearly conveyed the message that if a White man was with Black females, it must be for some sordid, deviant purpose. While the uncommonness of cross-racial interactions between White males and Black female feeds presumptions of sexual deviancy in instances like my experience with Glenda and Jamila, such presumptions also contribute to the rarity of such cross-racial interactions, as people try to avoid potential scrutiny, harassment, and stigma.

While I cannot generalize from all of my experiences with Black people and claim that all people in Black–White groups are perceived and treated in the same exact ways when interacting with other people in different social contexts, my experiences nevertheless provide a window into understanding some of the dynamics that shape how those in such mixed-race groups are perceived and treated when they are in certain spaces and engaged in certain activities. My experiences have made me pay much closer attention to how other Black–White groups are treated out in the world, and from what I have observed, the treatment appears to be consonant with what my Black friends and I have confronted.

Promoting healthier cross-racial interactions between Black and White people

Due to the legacy of over four centuries of highly problematic interactions between Black and White people in the United States, promoting healthy interactions and relationships between these two categories of people remains a significant challenge. The cumulative distrust between Blacks and Whites resulting from this legacy often precludes any attempts to forge cross-racial ties. The challenge of establishing such ties is exacerbated by the continuing high degree of racial residential and school segregation in the US, the enormous racial wealth gap between Blacks and Whites, social norms that discourage cross-racial interactions, media and politicians who purposefully try to divide people racially for their own self-serving interests, and efforts to pretend that we have a colorblind society.

My interactions with young Black persons have provided me with some insights on how to promote healthier, more meaningful interactions between White and Black people. For starters, people have to be willing to get out of their comfort zone and be open to getting to know people with whom they have little to no familiarity. To reach out to people outside of one's comfort zone necessitates not being afraid of being vulnerable and making mistakes. Over the years, I have inadvertently said things to Black people that were, in retrospect, naive, misguided, and stereotypical. These statements or questions were based on my limited experience and understanding at the time. In trying to establish cross-racial ties, people cannot expect to be infallible. People will make mistakes, but the key is to acknowledge them, learn from them, and do better the next time.

Another important prerequisite for establishing healthier cross-racial interactions is a willingness to "meet people halfway". This means that both White and Black people need to make an effort to understand, accommodate, and validate their respective cultural behaviors, styles, and traditions. The majority of White people I have observed expect Black people to unilaterally assimilate to White cultural standards. This "one-way street" approach prevents the formation of connections based on mutual respect.

In meeting people halfway, it is important to be authentic. If people try to present themselves as something that they are not, it comes across as insincere and phony. Trying to connect to people in another racial category through stereotypes associated with that category comes across as particularly offensive, as it reduces every person to a category.

Honesty is another important trait in meeting people halfway. White people have to acknowledge the existence of continuing racially disparate treatment in this society rather than pretending that our society is colorblind. To deny the reality of racially disparate treatment amounts to a microaggression, which in turn will make the possibility of establishing meaningful connections with Black people virtually impossible. The trick is to acknowledge the reality of race as a social category and the way it continues to shape people's lives but to also strive to treat people as unique individuals. This amounts to what seems to be a contradictory enterprise—simultaneously seeing and not seeing race.

A major prerequisite for establishing healthy cross-racial ties is to empathically listen to and validate each other's experiences. People cannot assume that their experiences are the same as other people's experiences and casually dismiss these latter experiences. Dismissing others' experiences as misinterpretations or overreactions only creates a wedge between people. In engaging in such empathic listening, it is important to exhibit humility. People need to acknowledge that they do not know everything, and that they have something valuable to learn from others who have had different experiences in life.

Another critical prerequisite for establishing healthy cross-racial ties is self-awareness and self-reflection. It is important to be self-aware and reflective of one's own status and behavior as well as the power dynamics in a particular situation. For instance, people should reflect on how they may unintentionally silence and disempower others in a social situation. I have become more mindful of how I, as a White person, may inadvertently reinforce racially skewed power imbalances by speaking too much and not listening enough to Black and other people of color in a particular social context.

As a White person who has had extensive involvement with Black children and adolescents, I also am mindful of trying to not come across as some type of "White savior". Interactions with young people should always be about them and building up their confidence in themselves to match or exceed the intellect and accomplishments of their adult mentors and tutors. If I, as a White person, inadvertently communicate to Black children that I am something so different from themselves and what they can become, it can actually undermine the children's ability to grow and develop intellectually.

In addition to being critically self-reflective, it is also important to be a critical observer of social life. People should look at a particular social setting and ask, "What is wrong with this picture?" "Who is missing, and why are they not here?" Observing and reflecting on the racial mix in a particular situation makes it possible to have some understanding of how underrepresented people might feel unwelcome and uncomfortable in that setting. In turn, such awareness makes it possible to then reconfigure social settings to make them more welcoming spaces. Such reconfigured settings then provide a more conducive environment for establishing positive cross-racial connections.

Learning objectives
Developing critical awareness of race privilege
The reader will become aware of and be able to critically analyze race privilege.

- Identify some of the obstacles that people face based on being identified as Black.
- Identify some of the ways life is easier for those designated as White.

Understanding ways of improving Black–White relations

The reader will be able to understand and articulate some of the ways of potentially improving interactions and relations between Black and White people.

- Explain the role of empathetic listening in cross-racial interactions.
- Explain the significance of meeting people of another race "part way".

Recommended projects and assignments

1. **Reflection assignment on portrayals of Blacks and Whites in school**:

   For this assignment, you will reflect on what you learned in school about Black and White people respectively. What were you taught about White people in school between kindergarten and 12th grade? How did teachers portray White people? What were you taught about Black people in school? How did teachers portray Black people? How do these presentations of White and Black people compare to those described by the author?

2. **Reflection assignment on the racial makeup of one's social network**:

   What is the racial makeup of your network of friends and extended family members? What accounts for this racial makeup? If people from some racial categories are underrepresented or missing, what might explain this? How might this racial makeup of your social network affect your own understanding of the world and of other people's experiences?

3. **Reflection assignment on the experiences of those not identified as "Black" or "White"**:

The author's experience largely involves contrasts between the experiences of Whites and Blacks. How do the experiences of Asians, Latinx persons, and Native Americans compare to Whites? What may account for any similarities? What may account for any differences? How do the experiences of Asians, Latinx persons, and Native Americans compare to Whites? What may account for any similarities? What may account for any differences?

4. **Research project on assumptions about guilt**:

    Review some data on wrongful convictions in the US (see, for example, The Sentencing Project at www.sentencingproject.org). How does this pattern tie into the author's accounts regarding guilt in Chapter 6? How do presentations of Black people in schools akin to those described by the author in Chapter 2 contribute to assumptions of Black guilt?

5. **Reflection assignment on racial privilege**:

    The author identifies a multitude of ways in which his life is easier as a White person. What are some of the things that could make it difficult for some White people to acknowledge such racial privileges? Why might people be more inclined to acknowledge privileges associated with ability or age than those associated with race?

Notes

1. Racial categories are capitalized throughout this book to signify how they are created and infused with meaning by people.
2. I use pseudonyms for the names of towns, schools, and people to protect the privacy of the people mentioned in this book.
3. Some of my classmates' families clearly appeared to be in the "poor" category based on the fact that they wore the same clothes to school and did not have enough money to buy or make their own Halloween costumes.
4. Interestingly, I was not friendly with either of the other two White students in the class. I had nothing to do with the other White boy in the class, who was the only person in the class whom I disliked and the only person whose name I have forgotten. I also did not interact with my only White female classmate, Olga, who was an immigrant from Portugal who spoke virtually no English.
5. I have met some White academics who do excellent work on race yet remain largely detached from people of color in their personal lives.
6. I discuss the significance of my relationship with my godchildren in Chapter 3.
7. I address Rennie and Coleman's experiences with police in Chapter 5.
8. I suggest in Chapter 2 that based on this country's history, one could just as easily stereotype White people in all of these ways if one wants to play the stereotype game.

9. See Cirillo (2020) for a discussion of some of the people who have invoked the idea that the US is a colorblind society.

10. Throughout this book, particularly in Chapters 4 through to 7, I discuss racial patterns I have experienced, either firsthand or vicariously, or observed, about the differential treatment of Black persons and White persons across a variety of context. In discussing these patterns, I am not saying that all Black people experience being treated in a particular way, or that all White people experience being treated in another way, or that all Black people treat a particular category of people in one way and all White people treat people in that category in a different way. Rather, I am alluding to empirical observations that suggest people in a particular racial category are significantly more likely to be treated differently than people in another racial category, or that people in a particular racial category generally treat people assigned to different racial categories differently. Talking about racial patterns means that there is something socially significant at play—due to a person's race that person is facing different assumptions, opportunities, sanctions, etc. If race was not socially significant, then there simply would not be any patterns—everyone would have the same likelihood of being treated in the same way across every social situation.

11. For instance, in June 1987, when I was with sitting in a car outside of a convenience store with my friend Glenda and her friend Jamila, both of whom were Black, two White males pulled up in vehicle adjacent to ours and menacingly and sarcastically asked me, "Where'd you get those hoes?" The implicit message here was that it was dirty and deviant for a White male to be out with Black females, and that if I wanted to avoid such unwanted comments I should avoid being in public with Black women. I discuss this experience in more detail in Chapter 8.

12. For instance, when I took my godchildren Monique, Rennie, and Coleman to a restaurant for breakfast in an overwhelmingly "White" tourist town along the shore in South Jersey, the host's eyes rolled and he was very cold and

unfriendly in contrast to the pleasant demeanor that host exercised with White adults who were with White children. This host was implicitly communicating to me, "Why are **you** with these kids?" and "Why have you brought **them** here?"

13. I also have experienced negative responses from some Black people to my involvement with young Black children, but these responses of disapproval have usually been communicated to the children behind my back as opposed to the more directly confrontational responses of Whites. Some of these responses have stemmed from the fact that is unusual for a White adult to be involved with Black children in our society. In general, we are taught that we should not care about people outside of our racial "tribe". This makes it more likely that some Black people will see a White person's involvement with Black children as being odd or suspect and to question that person's motives (e.g. assuming that the person is some type of predator). In addition, some Black adults may resent a White person's involvement with Black children because it implicitly conveys to those adults that they are not equipped to handle or are not interested in being there for the Black children or that the White person is trying to be a "White savior" who makes them look and feel ineffectual and inferior (I revisit this "White savior" concept in Chapter 8). This was clear in the case of my godchildren Monique, Rennie, and Coleman, as some adult family members communicated to the children that I was trying to "show them up".

14. I am principally talking about educators' assumptions regarding intellectual/academic ability in Chapter 4, but this also includes other types of ability, such as athletic ability.

15. I only focus on omissions of Black culture and history in this book, but the history and culture of Native Americans, Asians, and Latinx persons also were systematically ignored and excluded from the curriculum in all the schools I attended. In particular, unconscionable policies and practices that White Americans directed at Asians, Latinx persons, and Native Americans generally were left out of the curriculum or only

mentioned in passing. For example, we learned nothing about how racist US immigration laws excluded Asians for much of the US's history (Hipsman and Meissner, 2013), or how naturalization laws required applicants to demonstrate that they were "White" in order to become a naturalized citizen (Haney Lopez, 1997). We learned nothing about how between 1819 and 1969 the US government ripped Native American children from their families and forced them to attend government- or church-operated boarding schools, where these children encountered extensive physical, sexual, and emotional abuse and over 500 of them died as part of the government's effort to "assimilate" Native Americans to White cultural standards (Spring, 2021; Waxman, 2022). We also learned nothing about how over a million people of Mexican descent were deported to Mexico in the 1930s regardless of their citizenship status (Balderrama and Rodriguez, 2006). Although we did address some unconscionable episodes involving people who were members of these other pan-ethnic categories, such as forced removal of Native Americans and the "Trail of Tears" in the nineteenth century, and the internment of Japanese Americans during the Second World War, these episodes were mentioned ephemerally and, as noted in footnote 3, presented in a highly sanitized fashion. Similar to the presentation of Blacks, those belonging to the Asian, Latinx, and Native American categories appeared fleetingly on rare occasions during my 13 years of schooling and then would effectively disappear.

16. The "Draft Riots" in New York City in 1863 was brought up in passing by one teacher, but only for the purpose of addressing some Northern opposition to the Civil War. This teacher omitted that these riots involved Whites violently assaulting and murdering Blacks (Strausbaugh, 2016).

17. The sanitization of European Americans' treatment of Blacks was paralleled by the sanitization of European Americans' genocide, land theft, and displacement of millions of indigenous people (Race: The Power of an Illusion, 2003). Educators hid the sadistic violence and rapacious greed

for land that characterized this genocide of native people through a series of lies and distortions, including the idea that native people voluntarily gave up their land, few native people died, and any violence by European-Americans was in response to Native American aggression and violence (akin to someone initiating a violent encounter today and then invoking the "stand your ground" doctrine). Moreover, educators helped to legitimize this mass murder and theft of indigenous people through an uncritical presentation of the concept of Manifest Destiny, which I discuss later in Chapter 2. Educators also sanitized the internment of Japanese Americans by omitting how those interned were held at gunpoint in concentration camp-like conditions, had all of their possessions permanently seized by the government, and were held without one shred of evidence of any collaboration with the Japanese government.

18. The omission of any discussion of captors' systemic rape of enslaved Black women and the terror enslaved persons experienced in worrying about captors violating their bodies was part of the myth that we learned about "house slaves" having a more desirable situation than "field slaves". While enslaved persons who labored in the fields endured excruciating conditions that physically wreaked havoc on their bodies, enslaved persons who worked in their captors' homes were more likely to be subject to sexual violence (Turner and Machado, 2019).

19. Enslaved people, either individually or collectively, creatively worked with whatever means they had available to them to resist bondage and seek freedom (Turner and Machado, 2019). Some secretly found ways to learn to read notwithstanding laws preventing enslaved persons from becoming literate, some escaped, some became activists who joined abolitionist movements, wrote books, and gave public lectures about their experiences in bondage, and others led or participated in violent rebellion against their captors and other slaveholders (Blassingame, 1979; James, 1969; Turner and Machado, 2019).

20. I still encounter many people today in the 2020s who mistakenly understand racism as an individual problem rooted in prejudice. This suggests that our educational system has not improved much since the early 1980s.
21. We were not taught that there was a notable exception to the Thirteenth Amendment's prohibition of slavery—that those convicted of a crime could be forced to engage in slave labor by the State.
22. For instance, on May 13, 1960, six years after the *Brown v. Board of Education* decision, South Carolina's legislature passed a bill to preserve school segregation and thwart Black citizens' attempts to integrate public schools by suing through the federal courts (Equal Justice Initiative, 2023). On its face, the bill appeared to repeal language from a long-standing law that proclaimed that the state would provide funding to "racially segregated schools only" (id.). However, the bill was a deceptive maneuver designed to make it look like the legislature was opening the door for racial integration, when in fact the bill did nothing to invalidate another state law that mandated the closure of any Whites-only school that admitted a Black student (id.).
23. The FBI's Counter-Intelligence Program, better known as COINTELPRO, involved a series of covert, formal, illegal operations intended to monitor, control, disrupt, discredit, and destroy various disfavored political organizations within the United States between 1956 and 1971 (Cole, 2003; Perkus, 1976).
24. Anderson (2016) discusses a number of these racially coded strategies, including the Southern Strategy and the War on Drugs. The Southern Strategy, which has been employed by some Republican politicians starting with Richard Nixon in 1968, is an electoral strategy designed to increase political support among White voters by stoking these voters' fears of and prejudice against Blacks through racially coded appeals (e.g. clamping down on crime). The War on Drugs has been a vehicle through which federal, state, and local law

enforcement has disproportionately targeted and decimated Black and Brown communities since 1973, notwithstanding government claims that this "war" is a race-neutral effort to eradicate the supply of drugs in the US (Alexander, 2010; Anderson, 2016).

25. Black Americans have been significantly more likely than White Americans to be exposed to environmental hazards, such as air pollution and proximity to hazardous waste facilities, throughout American history (Adisa-Farrar, 2023; Bervotiz, 2020; Villarosa, 2020).

26. When people argue that racism is over (see, for example, US Supreme Court Justice John Roberts' opinion in *Shelby County v. Holder*, 570 US 529 (2013)), they are typically referring to the end of blatant, visible racist policies and practices. This misses the fact that racism has morphed into subtle and covert policies and practices to get around laws that prohibit racial discrimination. For instance, much of the racial exclusion we see with respect to housing occurs through zoning laws that are race-neutral on their face (Massey et al., 2013).

27. The US Public Health Service Syphilis Study at Tuskegee Institute was conducted between 1932 and 1972 to observe the natural history of untreated syphilis in nearly 400 Black men (Washington, 2008).

28. Jefferson states in *Notes on the State of Virginia*, "I advance it therefore as a suspicion only, that the blacks, whether originally a distinct race, or made distinct by time and circumstances, are inferior to the whites in the endowments both of body and mind" (Jefferson, 1998, p. 141).

29. We incorrectly learned that all enslaved people were freed by Lincoln's September 22, 1862 Emancipation Proclamation (effective January 1, 1863), but the Proclamation only applied to enslaved people in states that were rebelling against the Union at that time (Lincoln, 1998).

30. In his fourth debate with Stephen Douglass in 1858, Lincoln remarked, "I will say then that I am not, nor ever have been in favor of bringing about in any way the social and political

equality of the white and black races" (Basler et al., 1953, p. 146). Lincoln went on to state, "There is a physical difference between the white and the black races which I believe will forever forbid the two races living together... while they do remain together there must be the position of superior and inferior, and I as much as any man am in favor of having the superior position assigned to the white race" (id. at pp. 146–147).

31. There are a vast array of inventions by Black inventors that have improved the quality of life of Americans and made their lives easier, such as central heating, refrigerated trucks, the home security system, the three-way traffic signal, the mailbox, automatic elevator doors, the self-propelled street sweeper, the portable ironing board, the dry-scouring process for cleaning delicate clothing, the electret microphone, the carbon light bulb filament, the lawn sprinkler, ice cream, the cell phone, the touch-tone phone, and more recently the color IBM PC monitor and gigahertz chip (Greater Diversity News, 2016; Morgan, 2023; People of Color in Tech, 2022; Porter, 2023; Walker, 2023; Witter, 2021). Other inventions and innovations by Black inventors have been essential to Americans staying alive and healthy, including inoculation against smallpox, the process of separating plasma from whole blood, and more recently, the Laserphaco Probe for treating cataracts and the COVID-19 vaccine (Blakemore, 2021; Pilgrim, 2004; Romero et al., 2020; Witter, 2021).

32. This lack of context for the civil disturbance in cities in the 1960s is paralleled by the lack of context that *Fox News*, *Newsmax*, *One America News*, and other right-wing media outlets provided in covering the protests that occurred in the wake of the police murder of George Floyd in the late spring and summer of 2020. Rather than attempting to understand why disproportionately Black people were taking to the streets in 2020—to protest against long-standing police violence targeting Black people—these right-wing media outlets leapfrogged the issue of racially skewed police violence, and presented Black Lives Matter and other

protesters as engaging in wanton, purposeless violence and criminality out of the blue (see, for example, Norman, 2020).

33. I spent 4th grade through to 12th grade attending public schools in the upper-middle-class town of Helston. I do not recall ever seeing a Black student in any of Helston's schools between 1975 and 1984.

34. It is possible that my social class status made it easier to adopt a more sympathetic view towards Blacks. Although we would have been classified as working class when we lived in Longwood, by eighth grade my family had crossed into the upper-middle-class category. Being of upper-middle-class status made the gap between me and many Blacks in the US seem greater. Had I been of lower-class status when I was in eighth grade, I may have been more inclined to see my own White family as struggling, and perhaps would have been less open to being sympathetic toward Blacks.

35. All of the quotations presented in this book are recollections of what was said as close to verbatim as possible. I have kept a journal with observations of experiences since high school, and many of the quotations are culled from entries that were made into this journal soon after events happened.

36. The only thing I remember my tenth grade English teacher saying in passing before skipping the chapter on "Afro-American" writers was, "Richard Wright is kind of handsome, for a Black man". Besides the obvious demeaning implications of this statement, it reinforced the idea that Black people did not have much of importance to offer outside of the way they looked.

37. Our English literature textbook contained no readings by Asian, Latinx, or Native American authors.

38. This is consistent with DiAngelo's (2018) discussion of how many Whites try to shut down any discussions about race.

39. The 2020s anti-critical race theory (CRT) crusade against teaching about race and racism in schools that mostly White conservatives are waging can be understood in the

context of the miseducation that my peers and I received. Many of these anti-CRT crusaders are claiming that the presentation of this country's shameful racist history and the stories of people of color who have experienced racism amount to "indoctrination" (Balingit and Meckler, 2020; Gingrich, 2022). These White anti-CRT crusaders, like me, likely received a whitewashed education that severely downplayed racism and presented Whites as only good and benevolent. In addition, these crusaders likely have grown up in similar, largely segregated, insular "White" worlds and lack meaningful connections with Black people through which they could develop some vicarious understanding of Blacks' experiences. As a result, when these White anti-CRT crusaders are presented with information about race and racism that seeks to correct lies and distortions and teach people the truth about the profound role that race has played in shaping life outcomes, these crusaders are likely to dismiss such information because it appears so foreign and contradictory to what they have been taught. Many Whites' defensiveness and hostility when presented with this factually correct information is also likely rooted in how this revised, factually accurate information, throws in question their belief that their status and success in American society is solely due to their own efforts (see, for example, DiAngelo, 2018). When a non-whitewashed history of race and racism is taught, it becomes inescapable to deny that policies and practices have made life substantially easier and privileged for Whites compared to Blacks.

40. A well-orchestrated campaign since 2020 in Republican-controlled states such as Florida to ban books dealing with race and racism from school curricula and purge them from libraries reflects an authoritarian effort to remove such alternative opportunities and spaces. This modern censorship crusade is essentially about making sure that young people not only receive a fraudulent whitewashed presentation of this country's history and present, but also that these young people are denied any possible opportunities or spaces

that might lead them to question that distorted, inaccurate, homogenized presentation of the world.

41. The lack of racial diversity at Henderson was surprising to me when I arrived on campus, as both the College's promotional materials and its campus tour officials misrepresented the College's level of racial diversity.

42. While the fact that my friends and I shared the status of "college student" facilitated our ability to connect, the norm at that time was for White students to socialize and seek friendships with other White students and for Black students to socialize and seek friendships with other Black students. Black students on predominantly White campuses were more inclined to befriend White students due to the limited percentage of Black students.

43. I discuss this experience, which involved tutoring elementary children at a community center in Germantown, Pennsylvania, in the next subsection.

44. This situation involved a group of four students who were living below me blasting loud rock music all throughout the morning hours through paper-thin walls and yelling and singing as they got drunk and high on drugs. When I complained to my dean and other administration officials, they suggested that I wear earplugs or play soft music, and then left it up to me to arrange a meeting with these rowdy students. All through the process, College officials not only did nothing to assist me but also communicated to me that I was the one with the problem.

45. Observing other White people in comparison to myself, I have been struck by how often I have noticed over the course of my lifetime a degree of discomfort and awkwardness on the part of Whites when they interact with Black strangers. I have only experienced such discomfort and awkwardness when I have interacted with a minority of Black people who have expressed hostility and/or coldness to me from the get-go for some reason.

46. I met most of my friends through this form of networking. I met and became friends with Vernon through Calvin, and met and became friends with Jesse through Vernon. Likewise, I met Gianna, Carol, Tim, and Leon through Glenda.

47. This is not to say that what I learned in my classes did not also play a significant role in advancing my thinking about race and racism. Through sociology classes I learned to see race as a social construct, to distinguish between a capacity to perform and a particular performance, to see the many non-biological factors that shape performance, and to consider the political economy behind institutional policies and practices.

48. This point of self-reflection was brought into stark relief in the spring of 1987, when three Black male students from Stratford were wrongfully arrested in Philadelphia after police mistook them for several Black male suspects who allegedly had robbed a White female on a sidewalk at night near Preston University. The three Stratford students had gone to Preston to attend a party. Despite showing their college identification cards and having other people who could corroborate their alibis, the three students were detained in a holding cell for three nights before being released without charges. No apologies were issued.

49. Detractors of affirmative action in higher education never address the schooling advantages that White children have disproportionately enjoyed due to correlations between race and class as well as educators' discretionary decision-making (I discuss this decision-making in Chapter 4).

50. It was not clear how many people were living at Erin's row house, but it appeared that at least half a dozen extended family members were living with Erin, Erin's mom, and Erin's two siblings.

51. Due to the frustration I had with the Kids Connection program's unreliable transportation (the van always seemed to have problems or would be very late in picking us up), coupled with a desire to spend more time with my expanding

network of friends, I stopped tutoring in the Kids Connection Program after May 1986. When I was visiting Philadelphia with a friend in August 1994, I took a chance of swinging by Erin's mom's house, and was able to see and speak with Erin, who was then 17. Although I did not see Erin again, Erin's memory would be a guiding force in all my subsequent endeavors involving young Black persons.

52. The ABC program is a nationally based program that identifies and places high-performing middle and high school students of color in prestigious middle and high schools around the country.

53. Some argue that it is important for Black children to have same-race mentors and imply that White mentors will be less helpful because they will not be able to relate to the children and provide them with the validation and support that they need for healthy development (see, for example, Rhodes et al., 2006). While I agree that it is important, both symbolically and practically, to have mentors who are of the same race, I also believe that it is important to have caring White adult role models to counter the many uncaring White adults that these children will likely encounter.

54. This is not to say that there have not been times when I have taken brief refuge in Whiteness, but rather to say that my post-college experiences since 1993 prevent me from feeling comfortable or content in falling back on a White world devoid of racial concerns. As I discuss below, my experiences with my godchildren in particular preclude me from thinking about the world in nonracial terms. Whether it can be seen as a blessing or a curse, I am haunted by a piercing racial analysis of the world every single day.

55. My racial "re-education" in college had motivated me to pursue becoming a civil rights lawyer. To that end, I chose to go to CUNY Law School, a public interest-oriented law school that was dedicated to serving traditionally underrepresented, marginalized peoples. After graduating law school, I decided that I wanted to be more proactively involved with young

people and entered and completed a master's in education teacher certification program. Nevertheless, my law school experience, which included an "equality concentration" and an internship with the NAACP Legal Defense Fund, expanded my knowledge about the history of racial discrimination and sharpened my thinking regarding how the law had and had not responded to this discrimination.

56. There were four women living at the facility when I began tutoring, three were Black, and one was White. I assisted two of the Black women residing at the facility in preparing to obtain their General Equivalency Diploma (which is the equivalent of a high school diploma).

57. As Tatum (2003) notes in *Why Are All the Black Kids Sitting Together in the Cafeteria*, Black young people increasingly find themselves turning to their Black peers for validation of experiences that they perceive as connected to their race as they move into adolescence because White peers cannot relate to those experiences and often respond in dismissive ways. This is exactly what my godchildren confronted, as many of their White peers thought they were overreacting to perceived racial slights, or these peers tried to explain or rationalize incidents as being about something other than race.

58. All of the skits we performed were humorous, based on different social and political issues, and poked fun at racism in some way. For example, we did a "Foxy News" skit that mocked the gleeful cheerleading of *Fox News* during the second Gulf War, a "Shrapnel Jacks" anti-war commercial skit featuring a soldier and a Condoleezza Rice look-alike, and a "Wonder Woman of Color" skit about a Black female superhero who defends innocent Black people targeted and harassed by the police. We talked about and wrote drafts of many other skits, such as "Bad Hair Day at Work", which is about a workplace that has a grooming code that requires employees to curl their hair, but we found it nearly impossible to get everyone together to produce these skits after everyone got busy with school, work, and other commitments.

59. In *The Negro Family: The Case for National Action*, which is commonly known as the Moynihan Report, Daniel P. Moynihan argued that Blacks' own defective cultural values were the principal cause of the rise in Black single-mother families, not structural factors related to employment and education (US Department of Labor, 1965).

60. For an excellent analysis of the connections between trauma and addiction, see the work of psychologist Gabor Mate (see, for example, *In the Realm of Hungry Ghosts: Close Encounters with Addiction*).

61. The places I visited with my godchildren in the Washington, DC area included the National Children's Museum, the Smithsonian Institution, Wolf Trap National Park for the Performing Arts (both the Filene Center and the Children's Theatre-in-the Woods), International Day and concerts at the Lakefront Summer Festival in Columbia, Maryland, Harper's Ferry National Park, Shenandoah National Park, and a children's activity center in suburban Maryland.

62. I had developed a distrust of social workers based on some earlier encounters in my life as well as some articles I had read about social workers' greater proclivity to separate Black children from their families for relatively minor things. Also, I was familiar with some of the horrors of the foster care system and truly believed that my godchildren would experience irreparable harm if they were separated from each other and placed in foster care.

63. Based on numerous conversations with Black people of all ages as well as my own observations of social life, I have noticed that many Whites expect Blacks to assimilate to their standards, accommodate them, and make them feel comfortable.

64. Monique had become friends with Chante when Monique lived in Landon on and off between 1995 and 1997. By 1998, after years of transience, Monique and my godsons settled in Seeburg in Ocean County, where they finished the remainder of their schooling.

65. At the time, Chante was 14 years old, Tenaya was 8 years old, Jamil was 12 years old, and Cameron was 8 years old.

66. In particular, Chante and Tamika's grandfather began to hallucinate that I was having an affair with their grandmother and trying to take their grandmother away. I think the hallucinations reinforced their grandfather's more lucid objections to the idea of a White man interfering with the grandfather's control over the grandchildren.

67. After taking LSD in college, Evie's mother Shelly, who had been an honor's student, developed schizophrenia and lived in a facility separate from Evie for most of Evie's life until Shelly's death in 2015. Shelly was very appreciative of my involvement in Evie's life, and on one occasion when visiting, Shelly took me aside and asked me to look out for Evie if anything happened to Shelly.

68. For example, Estelle told me about an incident when a White woman publicly shouted at Estelle in a threatening manner for touching the oranges in a bin in the grocery store and then demanded that a clerk working at the store bring out some new oranges. Opal, who was the only Black person receiving dialysis treatment at a medical facility, shared complaining to the facility's staff after noticing being the only person whose dressing had not been cleaned. Deirdre, who had worked as a traveling nurse, shared stories with me about White patients who told Deidre that they did not want Deirdre touching them, or that they requested to Deirdre's supervisors that they wanted a White nurse. Opal, who had worked as a bank teller, also relayed similar stories about some White customers avoiding Opal in favor of White tellers or complaining to the bank manager behind Opal's back that they should not have a "colored" person working at the bank.

69. Deirdre recruited me to join her NAACP chapter in Ocean County and I am currently a member of that chapter.

70. In Chapter 4, I discuss Evie's exclusion from the College Prep English track and how her guidance counselor advised her to not take chemistry.

71. I address some of these subtle, hidden mechanisms in Chapters 4 through to 7.
72. I discuss some of these subtle mechanisms in more detail in Chapter 4.
73. I discuss these attributions in Chapter 6.
74. Rennie, Iggy, and Jared were placed in special education classes, but Peter, Kira, and Mick were not placed in special education classes after their parents vigorously battled with school officials to have them placed in higher ability classes. All six of these Black students later went on to graduate from college, contrary to the low expectations that educators held for them when they started school.
75. As discussed below, even high-achieving Black students were viewed as having suspect ability by educators when educators were not familiar with them.
76. Rennie's poor performance on this test was affected by the many days of school that Rennie had missed due to the instability of Deanna's situation.
77. Monique displayed greater resilience than Rennie and Coleman. Unlike Rennie and Coleman, Monique had some teachers who provided encouragement, and such encouragement likely assisted Monique in overcoming the difficulties posed by the instability of Monique's home life.
78. School officials eventually capitulated to Laura's complaints and restored the points to Henry's GPA. These officials told Laura that it was an accidental "computational error".
79. The underrepresentation of Black students in honors and AP classes was consistent with this alleged bargain with White parents. In general, despite making up roughly half of the CHS's student population, Black students accounted for only approximately ten percent of the students in honors classes, and only approximately five percent of the students in the AP classes during the 1995–1996 academic year.

80. Section 504 of the Rehabilitation Act of 1973 (29 USC. 794) states that "no qualified handicapped person shall, on the basis of handicap, be excluded from participation in, be denied the benefits of, or otherwise be subjected to discrimination under any program or activity which receives Federal financial assistance" (34 C.F.R. Part 104.4).

81. Under duress from me, Monique dropped out of the vocational program in tenth grade after two years. Had Monique remained in the program, it would have undermined Monique's chances to be accepted to college. In April 2023, Monique earned a dual PhD in social work and psychology from a prestigious university.

82. In order to work as a police officer, one must at least have a high school diploma or some equivalent credential. However, some police departments or federal law enforcement agencies may require applicants to have finished college coursework or a degree (Ingram, 2023).

83. Black students' average standardized test scores in reading and math fall below those of White students' average test scores at every grade level (see, for example, Assari et al., 2021; Drum, 2020).

84. I met Keenan in February 2023 through an event sponsored by the Thornton NAACP chapter to which I belong.

85. When Rennie confronted the White person with the video, this person did not apologize and tried to change the subject.

86. Rennie noted that other cyclists were playing music, and that he was playing his music at a lower volume than that of most of the other cyclists.

87. Del Toro and Wang (2021) found that 26 percent of the Black students received at least 1 suspension for a minor infraction over the course of the 3 years, compared with just 2 percent of White students. Minor infractions included things such as dress code violations, inappropriate language, or using a cell phone in class.

88. See, for example, Heyward and Max (2023).

89. Black people were nearly three times more likely than White people to be killed by police in 2023 (Mapping Police Violence, 2023).

90. Between 1982 and April 2023, 74 out of the 142 mass shootings in the US were carried out by White shooters (Statista, 2023).

91. Odawa officials' response to allegations of misconduct against White students generally has been more tempered and circumspect. For instance, when I inquired about a White male student who had been accused of raping an underage female, staff and administrators cautioned that we needed to be careful to not rush to judgment until a full investigation had been completed.

92. This psychological counselor, who was a friend of mine, knew that I had a history of advocating for students of color at the college and directed Halima to see me because Halima was in dire need of an advocate and the counselor could not fulfill this role.

93. This claim by Gondal was completely nonsensical in light of the fact that Halima had not attended the party.

94. Marion is the town in which the college is located.

95. The convictions would be removed from her record in five years if she had no subsequent convictions.

96. The Affirmative Action Officer had interviewed Gondal and found Gondal to have anger-related issues, as well as some apparent hostility to Black people. However, after Halima was forced into dropping the affirmative action complaint in order to get Gondal to drop his criminal complaint, these findings did not end up on Gondal's record, and Odawa did not pursue any further investigation into Gondal's conduct and mental fitness to be a campus safety officer.

97. My attempt to enlist the help of Odawa's only Black member of the Board of Trustees went nowhere, as he stepped down from his position a few days after I sent a letter.

98. I was not yet a tenured professor at the time that I took on the role of Halima's advocate.

99. The out of hand dismissal of Curt's and David's testimony raises an additional specter that Odawa staff and administrators did not see Black students' testimony as having any credibility.

100. As noted in Chapter 5, Curt indicated that Gondal regularly asked Black students for identification but did not make similar requests to White students.

101. See Burns (2011) for an in-depth discussion of the Central Park Five case.

102. Simmons was convicted of rape despite Simmons's jury being shown a lineup in which Simmons was the only one who was handcuffed and despite the victim's statement that "all n*****s look alike" (The Farm: Life Inside Angola Prison, 1998).

103. Media accounts of White male school shooters generally have examined these shooters' behavior through an environmental frame. For instance, articles about the 1999 Columbine High School shooters Eric Harris and Dylan Klebold frequently mentioned how these shooters had been bullied by classmates (see, for example, Conan, 1999).

104. One could argue that Gary's behavior should have been more harshly condemned because Gary brought a gun on school grounds.

105. A discreditable stigma is some deviant behavior or condition that is not yet known to others.

106. A discredited stigma is some deviant behavior or condition that is known to others.

107. It is not clear why only Evie and Fatima were summoned to the principal's office to discuss the video recording. It is possible that the White teacher who came into Evie's hotel room remembered seeing a Black female student holding a camcorder, and therefore did not ask Orrico to summon the two White female students who were in the hotel room with

Evie and Fatima. However, it is also possible that only Evie and Fatima were summoned because of an assumption on the part of the teacher and Orrico that the Black students were the "guilty" party in this instance.

108. Evie had shared information about her video recordings of the senior trip only with a handful of students and later surmised that this student must have learned about the video recordings through Orrico.

109. This is analogous to some police officers' efforts to demonize those who record problematic behavior by the police as a way of distracting attention from the substance of what the police themselves have done.

110. It is debatable whether Odawa administrators' actions at this event can be labeled as "unplanned". These administrators may have anticipated that students of color would talk about unpleasant experiences at Odawa and devised ways of subverting the discussion in advance of the event.

111. The demonization of Black victims by politicians and some media outlets has been common since the advent of Richard Nixon's "Southern Strategy" in the late 1960s. For instance, in the late 1970s and 1980s, poor Blacks were often disparaged through terms such as "welfare queen" (Denby, 2013) and "crackhead" (Blanchard, 2019), and in 2005, poor Black victims of Hurricane Katrina were demonized as "looters" (Kaufman, 2006; Lacy and Haspel, 2011). Over the past decade, it has become common in the wake of police killings of unarmed Black persons for the media to either demonize the victim (see, for example, Lipton, 2000; Taylor, 2006), or to bring up the non-sequitur distractor issue of "Black-on-Black crime" (see, for example, Suen, 2015). When America's ugly underbelly of race and class discrimination is exposed and becomes salient as a result of certain high-profile incidents like Hurricane Katrina or the police killings of Michael Brown, Eric Garner, and George Floyd, the demonization of Black victims helps to pull the rug back over this underbelly. Such demonization shifts attention

away from how institutionalized racism and other structural factors have contributed to Black victimization and helped to absolve Whites of any responsibility.

112. In addition to demonizing particular Black victims, I also observed instances in which some teachers, guidance counselors, and other staff members, particularly at RHS, blamed Black people in general for their plight. Consistent with Lewis's (1966) culture of poverty argument, these staff members adamantly claimed that Blacks' deficient cultural attributes—lack of work ethic, inability to save for the future, having too many babies out of wedlock—explained why a disproportionate percentage of Black people were struggling financially in the US. This victim-blaming rationale conveniently shifted attention away from ongoing institutionalized racial discrimination as well as the ways in which Whites have disproportionately benefited from government assistance in the not-so-distant past (for example, FHA and VA loans in the mid-twentieth century).

113. This is exactly what is happening in the 2020s, as some conservative White parents have complained that books or curricula that discuss anti-Black racism unfairly victimize them and their children (see, for example, Francis, 2023).

114. Some people, mostly White and mostly politically conservative, have objected to the term "privilege". These objectors deny that Whites enjoy any advantages in the US and/or argue that the term is divisive (see, for example, Bertram, 2020). Privilege simply refers to life being easier in some respects for people who have been assigned to a particular social category. For instance, life is easier to navigate for people who are between 5 feet and 6 and a half feet tall than it is for people who are less than 4 feet tall or over 7 feet tall because the built world has been created to accommodate people in the former size range. In general, people assigned the White racial category step into a world in which life is easier in some respects due to the way US society has been shaped by past and ongoing racial discrimination. White people benefit from this

discrimination regardless of how noble they might be on a personal level. For instance, ongoing racial discrimination by realtors, where they do not show Black and Brown people apartments and homes in certain neighborhoods and communities (see, for example, Choi et al., 2019), makes it easier for me as a White person to find an apartment or home. Likewise, ongoing racial discrimination in the appraisal of homes (Ostrowski, 2023) means that I can sell my home at a higher asking price than a Black person can for the exact same home. In both of these instances, I do not have to do anything to benefit from discriminatory actions that others have perpetrated at some point. "Privilege" is not a radical concept but rather honestly reflects the realities of a social world in which all people are not treated equally.

115. Although I encountered some teachers who did not communicate such expectations, the fact that I had other teachers who held high expectations neutralized the impact of the former.

116. These expectations also were likely shaped by my family's movement into the middle class after Longwood and upper-middle class by the time I reached middle school. Also, the expectations held for me were shaped by the norms of the communities that we lived in after Longwood. A majority of students in those communities did go on to college as opposed to going to vocational school, joining the military, or going straight into the labor market. However, a majority of the students at BHS, my godchildren's high school, also went on to college, yet teachers and guidance counselors did not see many of the Black children as "college material".

117. My apparent male sex designation also contributes to this perceived competence in the classroom. Those socially identified as "male" historically have been viewed as more competent than those socially identified as "female" regardless of actual level of competency.

118. When I was in law school, I had a Black male professor who always dressed in a three-piece suit. This professor became

upset with me and other students when we did not get dressed up for a presentation of briefs in a mock trial case. At the time, I did not appreciate why dress was so important to this professor. As a Black person who grew up in the 1960s in the South, this professor had encountered a world where Black people were generally treated disrespectfully. Dressing up for this professor and other Black people was a way to command some level of respect and dignity and be taken seriously.

119. It is possible that these directions-seekers approached me primarily because they felt more comfortable approaching me rather than because they saw me as knowledgeable.

120. There have been some instances in which I have been perceived as a threat. For instance, when I have been by myself in some settings (for example, parks) where young children are in proximity to me, parents have clutched or gathered up their children as if I were a potential child abductor.

121. Such preemptive maneuvers also are part of a calculated strategy to avoid possible unwanted, gratuitous encounters with police officers.

122. Coleman, Rennie, Jared, Maurice, and virtually every other young Black male I have known have been stopped at least once by police because they "fit the description" of a suspect for whom the police were searching.

123. Based on my voice, the judge likely inferred that I was White. Also, the judge was likely swayed by the fact that I was a college professor with a PhD.

124. Coleman's experience shows the linkage between macro-level institutional classism and racism and micro-level outcomes. Despite living approximately ten minutes away from a large high school in Thornton, Coleman and other middle and high school students from Seeburg, which has no high school of its own, had to catch a bus at 6:15 a.m. and go on an approximately 45-minute bus ride to reach BMS and BHS. Decades earlier Thornton had refused to

accommodate students from nearby Seeburg, ostensibly because it did not want the generally poorer students from Seeburg attending its middle and high schools. As a result, this meant that Seeburg students had to get up extra early to catch the bus to BMS. For Coleman, who worked a part-time job into the evening, this early departure time was difficult to meet. As a result, Coleman missed numerous days of school, which nearly led to him not graduating.

125. Coleman did not miss any more days of school and graduated that June.

126. We appeared to be selectively pulled over because we were doing the same speed as all of the other vehicles on that stretch of I-95.

127. Kevin, the White male boyfriend of my friend Marla, a Black woman, was stopped and questioned by police officers on multiple occasions when he was taking Marla's son Josh on the subway in New York City. Cedric, a White male married to a Black woman, was questioned about his relationship to his two biracial sons at two different airports.

References

Adisa-Farrar, T. (2023). How 600 years of environmental violence is still harming black communities. [Online] Earthjustice. Available at: https://earthjustice.org/article/overlooked-connections-between-black-injustice-and-environmentalism [Accessed 5 Apr. 2023].

Alexander, M. (2010). *The New Jim Crow: Mass Incarceration in the Age of Colorblindness*. New York, NY: The New Press.

Anderson, C. (2016). *White Rage: The Unspoken Truth of Our Racial Divide*. New York, NY: Bloomsbury.

Anderson, C. (2021). *The Second: Race and Guns in a Fatally Unequal America*. New York, NY: Bloomsbury.

Andrews, E. (2019). How many US presidents owned enslaved people? [Online] History. Available at: www.history.com/news/how-many-u-s-presidents-owned-slaves [Accessed 3 May 2023].

Assari, S., Mardani, A., Maleki, M., Boyce, S., and Barzargan, M. (2021). Black-White Achievement Gap: Role of Race, School Urbanity, and Parental Education. *Pediatric Health, Medicine and Therapeutics*. [Online] 12, pp. 1–11. Available at: www.ncbi.nlm.nih.gov/pmc/articles/PMC7797342/ [Accessed 18 Jun. 2023].

Baker, M., Bogel-Burroughs, N., and Marcus, I. (2022). Thousands of teens are being pushed into military's Junior R.O.T.C., *The New York Times*. [Online] Available at: www.nytimes.com/2022/12/11/us/jrotc-schools-mandatory-automatic-enrollment.html [Accessed 4 Jun. 2023].

Balderrama, F. E. and Rodriguez, R. (2006). *Decade of Betrayal: Mexican Repatriation in the 1930s*. Albuquerque, New Mexico: University of New Mexico Press.

Balingit, M. and Meckler, L. (2020). Trump alleges "left-wing indoctrination" in schools, says he will create national commission to push more "pro-American" history. *The Washington Post*. [Online] Available at: www.washingtonpost.com/education/trump-history-education/2020/09/17/f40535ec-ee2c-11ea-ab4e-581edb849379_story.html [Accessed 7 Apr. 2023].

Banerjee, A. and Johnson, C. (2020). African American workers built America. [Online] Center for Law and Social Policy. Available at: www.clasp.org/blog/african-american-workers-built-america/ [Accessed 3 May 2023].

Basler, R. P., Pratt, M. D., and Dunlap, L. A., eds. (1953). *Collected Works of Abraham Lincoln*. New Brunswick, NJ: Rutgers University Press.

Bellamy, C. (2023). A deadly massacre of the post-slavery era finally gets a suitable memorial. [Online] NBC News. Available at: www.nbcnews.com/news/nbcblk/colfax-massacre-monument-150th-anniversary-ceremony-rcna79151 [Accessed 26 Mar. 2023].

Berkovitz, C. (2020). Environmental racism has left Black communities especially vulnerable to COVID-19. [Online] The Century Foundation. Available at: https://tcf.org/content/commentary/environmental-racism-left-black-communities-especially-vulnerable-covid-19/ [Accessed 9 May 2021].

Bertram, C. (2020). On an objection to the idea of "White privilege". [Online] Crooked Timber. Available at: https://crookedtimber.org/2020/08/27/on-an-objection-to-the-idea-of-white-privilege/ [Accessed 19 Jun. 2023].

Blackmon, D. A. (2008). *Slavery by Another Name: The Re-Enslavement of Black Americans from the Civil War to World War II*. New York, NY: Anchor Books.

Blakemore, E. (2021). How an enslaved African man in Boston helped save generations from smallpox. [Online] History. Available at: www.history.com/news/smallpox-vaccine-onesimus-slave-cotton-mather [Accessed 10 May 2023].

Blanchard, S. K. (2019). "Crackhead" is an anti-Black pejorative, period. [Online] Filter. Available at: https://filtermag.org/crackhead-is-an-anti-black-pejorative-period/ [Accessed 8 Jun. 2023].

Blassingame, J. W. (1979). *The Slave Community: Plantation Life in the Antebellum South*. Rev. and enl. ed. New York, NY: Oxford University Press.

Brodkin, K. (1998). *How Jews Became White Folks and What That Says About Race in America*. New Brunswick, NJ: Rutgers University Press.

Brown, D. L. (2018). "Barbaric": America's cruel history of separating children from their parents. *The Washington Post*. [Online] Available at: www.washingtonpost.com/news/retropolis/wp/2018/05/31/barbaric-americas-cruel-history-of-separating-children-from-their-parents/ [Accessed 27 Apr. 2023].

Burns, S. (2011). *The Central Park Five*. New York, NY: Vintage Books.

Byrd, W. M. and Clayton, L. A. (2001). Race, Medicine, and Health Care in the United States: A Historical Survey. *Journal of the National Medical Association*, 93(3 Suppl), pp. 11S–34S. Available at: www.ncbi.nlm.nih.gov/pmc/articles/PMC2593958/ [Accessed 14 May 2023].

Carr, S. (2012). In Southern towns, "segregation academies" are still going strong. *The Atlantic*. [Online] Available at: www.theatlantic.com/national/archive/2012/12/in-southern-towns-segregation-academies-are-still-going-strong/266207/ [Accessed 8 May 2023].

Choi, A., Herber, K., and Winslow, O. (2019). Long island divided. *Newsday*. [Online] Available at: https://projects.newsday.com/long-island/real-estate-agents-investigation/ [Accessed 15 Jun. 2023].

Cirillo, F. J. (2020). Colorblindness has become a conservative shield for racial inequality. *The Washington Post*. [Online] Available at: www.washingtonpost.com/outlook/2020/08/07/colorblindness-has-become-conservative-shield-racial-inequality/ [Accessed 4 Apr. 2023].

Clotfelter, C. T., Ladd, H. F., and Vigdor, J. L. (2015). Public universities, equal opportunity, and the legacy of Jim Crow: Evidence from North Carolina. [Online] National Bureau of Economic Research. Available at: www.nber.org/papers/w21577 [Accessed 9 Apr. 2023].

Cole, D. (2003). *Enemy Aliens: Double Standards and Constitutional Freedoms in the War on Terrorism*. New York, NY: The New Press.

Conan, N. (1998). "Columbine" debunks the myths of the massacre. [Online] NPR. Available at: www.npr.org/transcripts/103287016 [Accessed 9 Jun. 2023].

Degruy, J. A. (2017). *Post Traumatic Slave Syndrome: America's Legacy of Enduring Injury and Healing*. Portland, OR: Joy Degruy Publications Inc.

Del Toro, J. and Wang, M. (2021). The Longitudinal Inter-Relations Between School Discipline and Academic Performance: Examining the Role of School Climate. *American Psychologist*. Available at: www.apa.org/news/press/releases/2021/10/black-students-harsh-discipline [Accessed 8 May 2023].

Demby, G. (2013). The truth behind the lies of the original "welfare queen". [Online] NPR. Available at: www.npr.org/sections/codeswitch/2013/12/20/255819681/the-truth-behind-the-lies-of-the-original-welfare-queen [Accessed 19 Jun. 2023].

DiAngelo, R. (2018). *White Fragility: Why It's So Hard for White People to Talk About Racism*. Boston, MA: Beacon Press.

Drum, K. (2020). Fact of the day: The Black-White education gap. *Mother Jones*. [Online] Available at: www.motherjones.com/kevin-drum/2020/09/fact-of-the-day-the-black-white-education-gap/ [Accessed 8 Apr. 2023].

Edelstein, D. (2018). Cincinnati race riots (1836). [Online] BlackPast. Available at: www.blackpast.org/african-american-history/cincinnati-race-riots-1836/ [Accessed 30 Mar. 2023].

Equal Justice Initiative. (n.d.). *South Carolina passes bill to maintain school segregation six years after Brown v. Board decision struck it down.* [Online] Available at: https://calendar.eji.org/racial-injustice/may/13 [Accessed 8 May 2023].

Flanagin, J. (2015). For the last time, the American Civil War was not about states' rights. [Online] Quartz. Available at: https://qz.com/378533/for-the-last-time-the-american-civil-war-was-not-about-states-rights [Accessed 29 Mar. 2023].

Francis, M. (2021). Two years before the Tulsa massacre, the "Red Summer" saw White mobs murder hundreds of Black Americans. [Online] Yahoo! News. Available at: https://news.yahoo.com/two-years-before-the-tulsa-massacre-the-red-summer-saw-white-mobs-murder-hundreds-of-black-americans-231429992.html [Accessed 29 Mar. 2023].

Francis, M. (2023). Who are "Moms for Liberty" and why is the group so controversial? [Online] Yahoo! News. Available at: https://news.yahoo.com/moms-for-liberty-controversial-school-book-bans-challenges-florida-politics-141208608.html [Accessed 19 Jun. 2023].

Gingrich, N. (2022). War on critical race theory: Gov. Noem emerges as national leader in fight against classroom indoctrination. [Online] Fox News. Available at: www.foxnews.com/opinion/critical-race-theory-gov-noem-classroom-indoctrination [Accessed 22 May 2023].

Goldberg, D.T. (1997). *Racial Subjects: Writing on Race in America.* New York, NY: Routledge.

González-Tennant, E. (2023). Remembering the Rosewood massacre. [Online] JSTOR Daily. Available at: https://daily.jstor.org/remembering-rosewood-massacre/ [Accessed 8 Apr. 2023].

Greater Diversity News. (2016). Henry T. Sampson created technology used in the first cell phone back in 1971 – gamma-electrical cell. [Online] Available at: https://greaterdiversity.com/meet-henry-t-sampson-man-created-first-cell-phone-back-1971/ [Accessed 5 May 2023].

Haney-Lopez, I. (1997). *White by Law: The Legal Construction of Race*. New York, NY: NYU Press.

Heyward, G. and Max, S. (2023). NYPD unit tasked with preventing gun violence illegally stops people at high rates, report finds. [Online] Gothamist. Available at: gothamist.com/news/nypd-unit-tasked-with-preventing-gun-violence-illegally-stops-people-at-high-rates-report-finds [Accessed 17 May 2023].

Hipsman, F. and Meissner, D. (2013). Immigration in the United States: New economic, social, political landscapes with legislative reform on the horizon. [Online] Migration Policy Institute. Available at: www.migrationpolicy.org/article/immigration-united-states-new-economic-social-political-landscapes-legislative-reform [Accessed 10 Mar. 2023].

Ingram, J. (2023). 25 best jobs that don't require a college degree. *US News*. [Online] Available at: money.usnews.com/money/careers/slideshow/25-best-jobs-that-dont-require-a-college-degree?slide=12 [Accessed 18 May 2023].

Irving, D. (2023). What would it take to close America's Black-White wealth gap? [Online] Rand Corporation. Available at: www.rand.org/blog/rand-review/2023/05/what-would-it-take-to-close-americas-black-white-wealth-gap.html [Accessed 27 May 2023].

James, C. L. R. (1969). *A History of Pan-African Revolt*. 2nd ed. Washington, DC: Drum and Spear Press.

Januta, A., Chung, A., Dowdell, J., and Hurley, L. (2020). Color of suspicion: Challenging police violence … while Black. [Online] Reuters. Available at: www.reuters.com/investigates/special-report/usa-police-immunity-race/ [Accessed 22 Feb. 2023].

Jefferson, T. (1998). *Notes on the State of Virginia*. New York, NY: Penguin Books.

Kamenetz, A. (2018). "Lies my teacher told me," and how American history can be used as a weapon. [Online] NPR. Available at: www.npr.org/2018/08/09/634991713/lies-my-teacher-told-me-and-how-american-history-can-be-used-as-a-weapon [Accessed 23 Mar. 2023].

Katznelson, I. (2006). *When Affirmative Action Was White: An Untold History of Racial Inequality in Twentieth-Century America*. New York, NY: W.W. Norton.

Kaufman, S. (2006). The criminalization of New Orleanians in Katrina's wake. [Online] Social Services Research Council. Available at: https://items.ssrc.org/understanding-katrina/the-criminalization-of-new-orleanians-in-katrinas-wake/ [Accessed 19 Jun. 2023].

Kroger, J. (2022). The end of affirmative action. *Inside Higher Ed*. [Online] Available at: www.insidehighered.com/blogs/leadership-higher-education/end-affirmative-action [Accessed 17 Jun. 2023].

Lacy, M. G. and Haspel, K. C. (2011). Apocalypse: The media's framing of Black looters, shooters, and brutes in Hurricane Katrina's aftermath. In: M. G. Lacy and K. A. Ono, eds., *Critical Rhetorics of Race*. New York, NY: NYU Press, pp. 21–46.

Lewis, O. (1966). The Culture of Poverty. *Scientific American*, 215(4), pp. 19–25.

Lincoln, A. (1998). *The Emancipation Proclamation*. Bedford, MA: Applewood Books.

Lipsitz, G. (1995). The Possessive Investment in Whiteness: Racialized Social Democracy and the "White" Problem in American Studies. *American Quarterly* 47(3), pp. 369–387.

Lipton, E. (2000). Giuliani cites criminal past of slain man. *New York Times*. [Online] p. B1. Available at: www.nytimes.com/2000/03/20/nyregion/giuliani-cites-criminal-past-of-slain-man.html [Accessed 19 Jun. 2023].

Loewen, J. (2005). *Sundown Towns: A Hidden Dimension of American Racism*. New York, NY: The New Press.

Mapping Police Violence (2023). Black people are 2.9x more likely to be killed by police than White people in the US [Online] Available at: https://mappingpoliceviolence.org/?gclid=Cj0KCQjw1rqkBhCTARIsAAHz7K2L4EcmuEnonq80S-1y2ajKOrLyXRC0doy1uCP_PD-BS_M9y2rSQPsaAuygEALw_wcB [Accessed 18 Jun. 2023].

Massey, D. and Denton, N. (1993). *American Apartheid*. Cambridge, MA: Harvard University Press.

Massey, D. S., Albright, L., Casciano, R., and Derickson, E. (2013). *Climbing Mount Laurel: The Struggle for Affordable Housing and Social Mobility in an American Suburb*. Princeton, NJ: Princeton University Press.

Mate, G. (2010). *In the Realm of Hungry Ghosts: Close Encounters with Addiction*. Berkeley, CA: North Atlantic Books.

Mineo, L. (2021). Racial wealth gap may be a key to other inequities. [Online] Harvard Gazette. Available at: https://news.harvard.edu/gazette/story/2021/06/racial-wealth-gap-may-be-a-key-to-other-inequities/ [Accessed 7 Apr. 2023].

Morgan, T. (2023). 8 black inventors who made daily life easier. [Online] History. Available at: www.history.com/news/8-black-inventors-african-american [Accessed 4 May 2023].

Mosvick, N. (2021). *Looking back at the Ku Klux Klan Act*. [Blog] Constitution Daily Blog. Available at: https://constitutioncenter.org/blog/looking-back-at-the-ku-klux-klan-act [Accessed 22 Mar. 2023].

Muhammad, K. G. (2010). *The Condemnation of Blackness: Race, Crime, and the Making of Modern Urban America*. Cambridge, MA: Harvard University Press.

Norman, G. (2020). Rioting, looting linked to George Floyd protests leaves trail of destruction across American cities. [Online] Fox News. Available at: www.foxnews.com/us/george-floyd-protests-aftermath [Accessed 9 May 2023].

Oluo, I. (2018). *So You Want to Talk About Race*. New York, NY: Seal Press.

Ostrowski, J. (2023). The Black neighborhood home appraisal gap is real and persistent. [Online] Bankrate. Available at: https://finance.yahoo.com/news/black-neighborhood-home-appraisal-gap-164515735.html [Accessed 19 Jun. 2023].

People of Color in Tech. (2022). Who is Shirley Ann Jackson, the African-American who invented the technology responsible for the touch-tone phone. [Online] Available at: https://peopleofcolorintech.com/front/who-is-shirley-ann-jackson-the-african-american-woman-who-invented-the-technology-responsible-for-the-touch-tone-phone/ [Accessed 5 May 2023].

Perkus, C. (1976). Preface. In N. Blackstock, ed., *COINTELPRO: The FBI's Secret War on Political Freedom*. New York, NY: Random House, pp. vii–xii.

Pilgrim, D. (2004). The truth about the death of Charles Drew. [Online] Ferris State University. Available at: https://jimcrowmuseum.ferris.edu/question/2004/june.htm [Accessed 23 Apr. 2023].

Pilgrim, D. (2012). What was Jim Crow. [Online] Ferris State University. Available at: www.ferris.edu/HTMLS/news/jimcrow/what.htm [Accessed 23 Apr. 2023].

Pitts, L. (2021). Tulsa the site of just one of many race massacres—but let's not talk about them. *Miami Herald*. [Online] Available at: news.yahoo.com/tulsa-just-one-many-race-223414932.html [Accessed 29 Mar. 2023].

Porter, T. (2023). Black History Month: The father of ice cream. [Online] Frozen Dessert Supplies. Available at: https://frozendessertsupplies.com/blogs/news/black-history-month-the-father-of-ice-cream [Accessed 10 May 2023].

Race: The Power of an Illusion. (2003). Directed by L. M. Smith [Film]. San Francisco, CA: California Newsreel.

Rhodes, J. E., Reddy, R., Grossman, J. B., and Lee, J. M. (2006). Volunteer Mentoring Relationships with Minority Youth: An Analysis of Same-Versus Cross-Race Matches. *Journal of Applied Social Psychology*, 32(10), pp. 2114–2133.

Romero, L., Salzman, S., and Folmer, K. (2020). Kizzmekia Corbett, an African American woman, is praised as key scientist behind COVID-19 vaccine. [Online] ABC News. Available at: https://abcnews.go.com/Health/kizzmekia-corbett-african-american-woman-praised-key-scientist/story?id=74679965 [Accessed 18 May 2023].

Shafer, R. G. (2022). July Fourth parade led to a massacre of Black people in Hamburg, S.C. *The Washington Post*. [Online] Available at: www.washingtonpost.com/history/2022/07/04/hamburg-massacre-july-4/ [Accessed 18 Apr. 2023].

Shapiro, T. M. (2003). *The Hidden Cost of Being African American*. New York, NY: Oxford University Press.

Sherman, S. Y. (2022). Fighting for words, fighting for students. *Washington Informer*. [Online] Available at: www.washingtoninformer.com/fighting-for-words-fighting-for-students/ [Accessed 16 Apr. 2023].

Spring, J. (2021). *Deculturalization and the Struggle for Equality*. 9th ed. New York, NY: Routledge.

Statista. (2023). Mass shootings in the US by shooter's race/ethnicity as of April 2023. [Online] Available at: www.statista.com/statistics/476456/mass-shootings-in-the-us-by-shooter-s-race/ [Accessed 1 Jun. 2023].

Stephens, R. (2020). The truth laid bare: Lessons from Ocoee massacre. [Online] Pegasus. Available at: www.ucf.edu/pegasus/the-truth-laid-bare/ [Accessed 14 Apr. 2023].

Strausbaugh, J. (2016). White riot: Why the New York draft riots of 1863 matter today. [Online] Observer. Available at: https://observer.com/2016/07/white-riot-why-the-new-york-draft-riots-of-1863-matter-today/ [Accessed 13 May 2023].

Suen, B. (2015). Fox News revives "black-on-black crime" canard to dismiss Black Lives Matter movement. [Online] Media Matters. Available at: www.mediamatters.org/sean-hannity/fox-news-revives-black-black-crime-canard-dismiss-black-lives-matter-movement [Accessed 19 Jun. 2023].

Sugrue, T. J. (2005). *The Origins of the Urban Crisis: Race and Inequality in Postwar Detroit*. Princeton, NJ: Princeton University Press.

Tatum, B. D. (2003). *Why Are All the Black Kids Sitting Together in the Cafeteria?: And Other Conversations About Race*. New York, NY: Basic Books.

Taylor, K. Y. (2006). The shooting of Sean Bell and the resurgence of American racism. [Online] Counterpunch. Available at: www.counterpunch.org/2006/12/02/the-shooting-of-sean-bell-and-the-resurgence-of-american-racism/ [Accessed 19 Jun. 2023].

Tensley, B. (2021). America's long history of Black voter suppression. [Online] CNN. Available at: www.cnn.com/interactive/2021/05/politics/black-voting-rights-suppression-timeline/ [Accessed 4 Apr. 2023].

The Farm: Life Inside Angola Prison. (1998). Directed by L. Garbus and J. Stack. [Film] Los Angeles, CA: Seventh Art Releasing.

Turner, K. and Machado, J. (2019). 5 things people still get wrong about slavery. [Online] Vox. Available at: www.vox.com/identities/2019/8/22/20812883/1619-slavery-project-anniversary [Accessed 22 Mar. 2023].

US Department of Health and Human Services. (2006). Your Rights under Section 504 of the Rehabilitation Act. [Online] Washington, DC: US Department of Health and Human Services, pp. 1–2. Available at: www.hhs.gov/sites/default/files/ocr/civilrights/resources/factsheets/504.pdf [Accessed 26 Apr. 2023].

US Department of Labor. (1965). *The Negro Family: The Case for National Action*. Washington, DC: US Department of Labor, pp. 1–90.

Vendantam, S. (2007). In boardrooms and in courtrooms, diversity makes a difference. *The Washington Post*. [Online]. Available at: https://www.washingtonpost.com/archive/politics/2007/01/15/in-boardrooms-and-in-courtrooms-diversity-makes-a-difference/3ce467d4-3b71-4fd0-9782-9753ba227ae1/ [Accessed 27 Mar. 2023].

Villarosa, L. (2020). Pollution is killing Black Americans. This community fought back. *New York Times Magazine*. [Online] Available at: www.nytimes.com/2020/07/28/magazine/pollution-philadelphia-black-americans.html [Accessed 8 May 2023].

Walker, E. J. (2023). Black inventor Philip Downing is the reason for mailboxes and then some. [Online] The Black Wall Street Times. Available at: https://theblackwallsttimes.com/2022/02/18/black-inventor-philip-downing-is-the-reason-for-mailboxes-and-then-some/ [Accessed 5 May 2023].

Walvin, J. (2018). *Slavery: The History and Legacy of One of the World's Most Brutal Institutions*. Chicago, IL: Connell Publishing.

Washington, H. A. (2008). *Medical Apartheid: The Dark History of Medical Experimentation on Black Americans from Colonial Times to the Present*. New York, NY: Anchor Books.

Waxman, O. B. (2022). The history of Native American boarding schools is even more complicated than a new report reveals. *Time*. [Online] Available at: https://time.com/6177069/american-indian-boarding-schools-history/ [Accessed 19 Mar. 2023].

Wellman, D. (1993). *Portraits of White Racism*. 2nd ed. New York, NY: Cambridge University Press.

Witter, B. (2021). 10 black inventors who changed your life. [Online] Biography. Available at: www.biography.com/inventors/madam-cj-walker-black-inventors [Accessed 4 May 2023].

Recommended further reading

Alexander, M. (2010). *The New Jim Crow: Mass Incarceration in the Age of Colorblindness*. New York, NY: The New Press.

DiAngelo, R. (2018). *White Fragility: Why It's So Hard for White People to Talk About Racism*. Boston, MA: Beacon Press.

McGhee, H. (2021). *The Sum of Us: What Racism Costs Everyone and How We Can Prosper Together*. New York, NY: One World.

Oluo, I. (2018). *So You Want to Talk About Race*. New York, NY: Seal Press.

Tatum, B. D. (2003). *Why Are All the Black Kids Sitting Together in the Cafeteria: And Other Conversations About Race*. New York, NY: Basic Books.

Index

affirmative action 90

Blackness 3, 6, 9, 25, 29, 35, 47, 52, 59–60, 101–102, 123, 128, 136, 139, 143, 153, 155, 161–162, 179
   demonization 25, 35, 102, 153, 161
   devaluation 35
   lack of agency 25, 35
   marginalization 9, 25
   misinformation 3
   salience 143, 155, 179
   stereotypes 3, 6, 25, 101, 123, 128, 136, 139, 143, 162
   vicarious understanding of 29, 47, 52, 59–60

Black–White achievement gap 90

colorblindness 63, 137

consciousness, racial 5, 9, 41

cross-racial interactions 1–2, 4, 6, 36–38, 42, 119, 176, 189
   communication 46, 53, 57–58
   emotional connections 3, 36, 49, 51
   empathetic listening 46, 53
   facilitators of 37–39, 53, 62, 189
   friendships 1, 38–40
   normative expectations 4, 119
   opportunities for 5
   others' perceptions and treatment of 6, 176
   sense of kinship 50–52, 59

cultural capital 91

discretion 6, 63, 66, 81–82, 95, 97, 106–107, 109, 128, 132–134, 137, 139, 145, 161
   police 95, 97, 106–107, 109, 123, 128, 133, 145, 161
   school personnel 6, 66, 81–82, 123, 134, 137, 145
   security guards 139, 145
   store personnel 132

discrimination 109–110, 112, 123, 128, 132, 134
   civilians 117
   police 112, 114, 117, 123, 128
   school personnel 110, 115, 123, 134
   security guards 109, 113–114, 117

store personnel 132

expectations of ability and race 6, 63, 65
   college and career 81
   higher ability class placement 74
   lower ability class placement 66
   second chances 63

guilt of Blacks 6, 101, 127
   attributions of blame 101, 145

identity, racial 6, 9, 41, 164
inequality 90, 122, 148, 162
innocence of Whites 6, 149
   casual dismissal of racism 155
   covering up behavior 153
   rationalizations 155, 157
   shifting blame 153, 162
   silencing race 154–155

power, racial 6, 121, 176
   limits on power 176
privilege, racial 6, 41, 163

racial hierarchy 90, 154, 162

schema, racial 2

school 1, 3, 9, 37, 60, 110, 115, 134, 141, 153
   censorship of Black history and experiences 11
   discouragement by teachers 32
   framing of racism 18
   linear progress narrative 20
   minimization of racism 35
   miseducation 3, 9
   portrayals of Blacks 9, 25, 35
   portrayals of Whites 9, 23, 35
   punishment 110, 115, 134, 141
   re-education 37
   sanitization of racism 16, 153
   segregation 28
   silencing race 9
segregation, residential 3, 5, 28, 118
social control 99, 102, 109
   appearance and dress codes 109
   containment 105
   herding 103, 105
   surveillance 103, 105, 109

threat of Blacks 6, 93
   age 98
   gender 94
   in Black spaces 120

in racially mixed spaces 118
in White spaces 112
presence of Whites 121

volunteer experiences 31, 41

wealth gap, racial 90–91
Whiteness 6, 9, 23, 35, 41, 118–119, 121, 149, 163, 176
appeasement 119
benevolence 23

entitlement 118
innocence 6, 149
power 6, 121, 176
privilege 6, 41, 163
stereotypes 162
superiority 9, 23, 35
upstanding image 154
White fragility 154

www.ingramcontent.com/pod-product-compliance
Lightning Source LLC
Chambersburg PA
CBHW070801230426
43665CB00017B/2442